Pearson's Canal Companion
WELSH WATERS

Troll Publishing Limited
32 Webb Ellis Industrial Park
Rugby, Warwickshire CV21 2NP
Tel/fax: 01788 546692
email: canalcompanions@trollpublishing.co.uk
Company Number 826713

Tillerman

Eight editions in twenty-seven years: you don't need to be a non-plussed GCSE Maths multiple-choice examinee to work out that, on average, every three and a half years or so, the author of this guide revisits the scene of the crime, so to speak, to see what fate and the authorities have managed to do with the canals of Wales in his absence. Though anticipated with something approaching pleasure, these sort of sentimental journeys can prove sobering experiences, akin to visiting an old friend parked in a lay-by on the outskirts of Dementia. It is in the nature of the canal network that time should treat it kindly, that its latent resonances be respected. But what do I find? A surge of new, off-line marinas, a palpable lack of paint, a plethora of signage - often inappropriate and ugly - deteriorating towpaths, and apparent inertia where the Montgomery Canal is concerned. It has always seemed to me ironic that the Llangollen - most popular canal in the country - is accompanied for much of its length by an indifferent towpath. Contrast its condition with the unnavigable Grantham Canal and see what is possible. It cannot be that expensive compared with invading Iraq. But - lest I descend into bathos - don't let me give you the impression that the canals contained within are somehow in irreversible decline: there's life in them yet and I have derived much pleasure in encountering them again. Whixall Moss, Frankton Locks, the Ceiriog Valley, those unearthly and as yet unrestored backwaters on the Monty, the Birmingham & Liverpool's slow loping stride across the unpopulated edge of Staffordshire: canal exploration, afoot or afloat, doesn't come much better.
Michael Pearson

Bridge 140, Montgomery Canal

f you are looking for a boating holiday you need look no further

Hire direct from the leading narrowboat operators with all boats inspected and awarded star ratings by Visit Britain.

fleet of over 200 boats for 2 to 12 people om 11 start bases throughout the UK so u can be sure of the widest choice.

eginners are welcome.

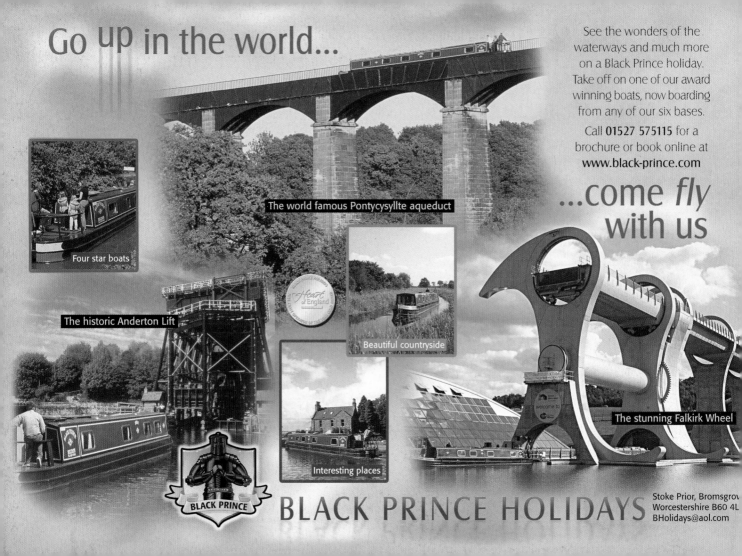

Countrywide Cruisers

Luxury holidays afloat

At Countrywide, the fine reputation which we now enjoy has been established with a fleet of narrowboats of exceptional comfort and reliability, built and operated by a team with a wealth of experience.

We turn round a maximum of five boats on any one day with the result that we are able to devote considerable resources to the cleaning and servicing of each one. Rest assured that you will take over an immaculate boat in the peak of operating condition.

Countrywide Cruisers (Brewood) Ltd,
The Wharf, Brewood, Staffordshire ST19 9BG
T: +44 (0)1902 850166 F: +44 (0)1902 851662
E: info@countrywide-cruisers.com
W: www.countrywide-cruisers.com

5

www.BoatingInEngland.co.uk

The Shropshire Union

DESPITE the proximity of Wolverhampton, Autherley, like many canal junctions, is self-contained. It is not pretty in a conventional sense, being bordered by housing estates, sewage plants and public open spaces. In typically pithy fashion, the old boatmen called it 'Cut End', for the obvious reason that the Shropshire Union Canal began and, more pertinently, ended here. Once there was all the paraphernalia of a meeting of waterways: toll office, stables, workshops, employees cottages, and a dominant, sweeping roving bridge carrying the Staffs & Worcs towpath over the entrance to the Shropshire Union. A stop lock - just six inches deep - protected the two companies' precious water supplies. Much of this infrastructure survives, enjoying a new lease of life in the leisure age as a hire base and boatyard. The 2008 Inland Waterways Association National Festival took place in the vicinity of Autherley and was deemed a huge success: over three hundred boats attended, as did two hundred and fifty exhibitors and twenty-four thousand visitors; evidence, surely, of the canal network's continuing appeal.

A massive sewage plant provides the canal with much of its water; suitably treated of course, or perhaps this explains the

Shropshire Union's apparent impatience to get on with its journey to the north-west. Whatever the motivation, Autherley is soon forgotten as the canal crosses the boundary between the West Midlands and Staffordshire and leaves the housing estates of Wolverhampton behind. The land east of the canal was once occupied by an aerodrome, whilst the works by Bridge 4 was formerly an aircraft factory, turning out, amongst other designs, the 'Defiant' fighter plane.

An 'invisible' aqueduct carries the canal over the little River Penk before the waterway goes through a series of contortions which see it narrowing, then widening, then narrowing again before resuming its usual width beyond Bridge 6. Temporarily, the M54 impinges, but otherwise the landscape is serene and unruffled, setting the scene for the forty mile journey to Nantwich through some unexpectedly remote countryside. Between bridges 4 and 7 the towpath forms part of 'The Monarch's Way', a circuitous 615 mile waymarked path inspired by King Charles II's escape route from Worcester to Shoreham-by-Sea in 1651.

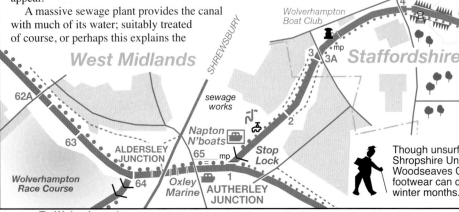

Though unsurfaced for a considerable proportion of its length, the Shropshire Union towpath (with the notable exception of Woodseaves Cutting - Map 7) can be comfortably walked, though footwear can quickly become wet and muddy, especially in the winter months. Cyclists may find the going bumpy in places.

THE Shropshire Union slices through the Staffordshire countryside in cuttings and upon embankments typical of the bold, 19th century designs of Thomas Telford, who engineered this route between Autherley and Nantwich, originally known as the Birmingham & Liverpool Junction Canal.

Travelling northwards you rapidly become attuned to the unique atmosphere of this canal. Far from becoming monotonous, its purposeful, loping stride across the landscape is strangely exhilarating, perhaps due to the recurring contrast of shadowy cuttings and panorama providing embankments, known as 'rockings' and 'valleys' respectively to past generations of boatmen.

a marauding panther.

North of Brewood, the canal crosses the old Roman Road of Watling Street on a sturdy, yet elegant aqueduct of iron, brick and stone construction: it occurs to us that some time has elapsed since it last benefitted from a coat of paint. Nearby Belvide Reservoir is another of the main sources of water supply for the Shropshire Union Canal. It is also, under the auspices of the West Midland Bird Club, a magnet for ornithologists. Broom Hall, east of Bridge 16, was the home of William Carlos who hid King Charles II in the oak tree at nearby Boscobel after the Battle of Worcester in 1651.

There are notable structures either side of Brewood. To the south the distinctly ornate, balustraded Avenue Bridge (No 10) carries the carriageway to Chillington Hall. The advent of the canals heralded many similar attempts at ornamentation and disguise, where powerful landowners would only condescend to permit a waterway to cross their parklands if suitable steps were taken to adorn the otherwise purely functional architecture of the new trade route. Chillington itself lies about a mile and a half to the west in grounds landscaped by Capability Brown. En route you encounter Giffard's Cross, where in the sixteenth century one of the Giffards (who have inhabited the estate for over eight hundred years) shot

Boatbuilding and maintenance is undertaken at Stretton Wharf, beyond which the canal is once more engulfed by one of its trademark cuttings. For a while activity on the towpath is augmented by walkers on the Staffordshire Way which seems to encounter a good many canals on its wanderings between Kinver and Mow Cop. Long term followers of the *Canal Companions* may care to learn that this very map was - way back in 1981 - the prototype from which all the maps in the series evolved. In its first guise it was hand drawn on cardboard, with a perspex flap for the second colour, and its lettering cut out and stuck on with gum; all a far cry from the Apple Mac which shoulders the work now!

for details of facilities at Brewood turn to page 10

Brewood

Map 2

Probably because it is so close to the county boundary, Brewood feels more like Shropshire; there being a 'West Country' richness about it that doesn't pertain, for example, to nearby Penkridge. And there really is a timelessness about 'Brood' which seduces you into spending longer here than you might have planned. Winding lanes of gracious houses lead to the old market place where the distinctive, and often venerable vehicles of the Green Bus Company pause before rumbling off in a cloud of blue smoke to Wolverhampton. Enhancing one corner of the square is 'Speedwell Castle', a Gothic fantasy erected in the 18th century on the winnings of a racehorse named Speedwell. The tall-spired parish church is notable for its Giffard family tombs, whilst the Roman Catholic church by Bridge 14 is the work of no less a Victorian architect than Augustus Welby Northmore Pugin.

Eating & Drinking

BRIDGE INN - Bridge 14. Tel: 01902 851999. Much extended former boatmans' pub. Marston's & guest ales. Home cooked food. *Good Beer Guide* entry. ST19 9BD

ADMIRAL RODNEY - Dean Street. Tel: 01902 850583. Homely pub in a handsome street. Good choice of food and real ales. ST19 9BU

THE MESS - Market Place. Tel: 01902 851694. Daytime cafe and evening restaurant. *www.the-mess.co.uk* ST19 9BS

THE CURRY INN - Church Street. Tel: 01902 850989. Eat in or take-away Indian. ST19 9BT

Shopping

Old fashioned shops where you can eavesdrop on local gossip: SPAR (with cash machine) and branch of Lloyds TSB Bank. COOPERS foodstore is excellent, as is the VILLAGE BAKERY for filled

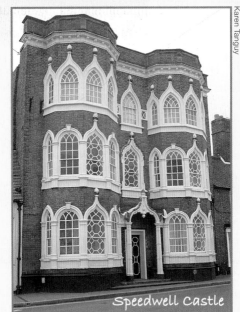

Karen Tanguy

Speedwell Castle

baps. Chillington reared beef and lamb from MAIDEN & SON butchers on Stafford Street.

Things to Do

CHILLINGTON HALL - about a mile and a half west of Bridge 10. Tel: 01902 850236. The imposing 18th century house (incorporating earlier structures) is open to the general public on Sunday afternoons in July and on Wednesday, Thursday, Friday and Sunday afternoons in August. The grounds (with lake and temples) are open daily from Easter until the end of May. WV8 1RE

Connections

BUSES - Hourly and endearing Green Bus Co services (Mon-Sat) to/from Wolverhampton; some run through to/from Wheaton Aston and are thus useful for one-way towpath walks. Tel: 0871 200 2233.

Wheaton Aston

Map 3

Once purely a farming community, Wheaton Aston has been overwhelmed by modern housing. So it's certainly no picture postcard village, but at least it appears to be thriving, defying the trend towards rural decline.

Eating & Drinking

HARTLEY ARMS - Bridge 19. Tel: 01785 840232. Canalside pub offering a range of food. ST19 9NF

COACH & HORSES - village centre. Tel: 01785 841048. Throwback Banks's local. Hot pork rolls. ST19 9NP

LUCKY HOUSE - High Street. Tel: 01785 841048. Chinese takeaway. ST19 9NP

Shopping

There's a small convenience store on the way into the village if you're in a rush, and a small post office (at the time of writing!) a bit deeper in, but the village's best shop is undoubtedly the SPAR opposite the church. It's open daily 7am-10pm and, along with all the other to be expected requisites, does a nice line in spit-roasted chickens, fresh-filled baguettes, and ready-to-eat pies and pasties: mind you you have to push past half the village in there gossiping to get to the counter! Turner's quaint canalside garage stocks Calor gas, diesel and boating accessories. Free range eggs from Bridge Farm.

Connections

BUSES - Services to/from Brewood, Wolverhampton. Tel: 0871 200 2233.

HEATON ASTON Lock is strangely solitary - the only one in twenty-five miles of canal; a telling measure of Telford's advanced engineering techniques. For about a mile the canal penetrates the deciduous heart of Lapley Wood, and there's another typical Shroppie cutting by Little Onn, but elsewhere the embankments offer wide views eastwards towards Cannock Chase; and beyond, perhaps, to a tell-tale plume of steam from Rugeley's power station.

How astonishingly remote and

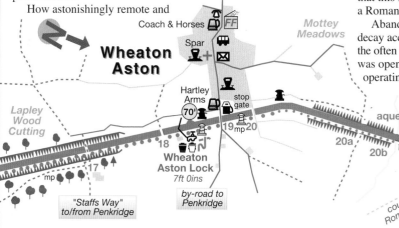

Wheaton Aston

Coach & Horses

Spar

Mottey Meadows

Hartley Arms

(70')

stop gate

Lapley Wood Cutting

18

17

mp

Wheaton Aston Lock
7ft 0ins

"Staffs Way" to/from Penkridge

by-road to Penkridge

19 mp 20

aqueducts

20a

20b

20c mp

stop gate

21

22

23 mp 24

Little Onn
Hall

former WWII aerodrome

course of Roman Road

Rye Hill Cutting

Sadly (though perhaps understandably) access is by permit only (Tel: 01743 282000) but those who do venture with authority into this unchanged landscape can encounter such rarities as the Horsetail Weevil and Snake's Head Fritillary, the latter at its most northerly discovered location.

One of the canal's lengthy embankments carries it across a sequence of culverts which provide access between neighbouring fields. It also spans a brook which flows eastwards into the River Penk, registering the fact that this is the watershed between the Trent and the Severn. The ghost of a Roman Road bisects the canal at the southern end of Rye Hill Cutting.

Abandoned wartime aerodromes inevitably have their ghosts, and in decay accumulate a patina of lore and legend, hard perhaps to equate with the often mundane use to which they were put after closure. Wheaton Aston was opened in 1941 and became one of the RAF's largest training units, operating a squadron of 'Oxfords'. There were at least two canal dramas:

unpeopled the landscape seems. The West Midlands conurbation is less than a dozen miles to the south, yet moor for the night between Wheaton Aston and Little Onn, and you'll have only the occasional eerie hoot of a hunting owl, or the distant silent wash of headlights on a country lane, for company. Something of this sense of isolation must explain the survival of Mottey Meadows, alluvial flood meadowlands, unploughed for centuries, whose name apparently derives from the French word for peat - *motteux*.

once an American 'Thunderbolt' crash-landed in the waterway. Another well remembered wartime incident occurred at the lock when a narrowboat, carrying an unsheeted cargo of shining aluminium on a moonlit night, was attacked by a German aircraft which unleashed a bomb that exploded less than a hundred yards from the chamber. After the war the aerodrome's inhospitable huts were used for some twenty years as a transit depot for displaced persons, primarily Poles; then the site became a pig farm!

Shelmore Embankment

12

THE buildings of two wharves remain intact at High Onn. One - now converted into a most desirable home - belonged to Cadbury's, the other to a local landowner, suggesting that there was once a degree of agricultural traffic on the canal. Deep shadowy sandstone cuttings, spanned by lichened grey stone bridges of simple balance and unaffected beauty, lead to the eighty-one unlined yards of Cowley Tunnel; the only one on the Shropshire Union. Once a dizzy jungle of trees darkened the approaches so much that you were never quite sure where the tunnel began and the cutting ended, but their roots caused instabilities in what was already a brittle rock strata and they were felled in 1985.

On a clear day the embankments north of Gnosall reveal that famous Shropshire landmark, The Wrekin, 15 miles to the south-west; a slumbering hunchback of a summit, 1335ft high. A. E. Housman celebrated it in *A Shropshire Lad,* and Salopians raise their glasses in a toast to: "All friends around the Wrekin".

Now in use as a public footpath, the dismantled railway line which crossed the canal at Gnosall once usefully connected Stafford with Shrewsbury until a certain Doctor made his presence felt. Historically it was unusual in that it was actually built by the Shropshire Union Canal Company, apparently hedging their bets on the transport mode of the future. When, in 1846, they leased themselves to the London & North Western Railway, few shareholders would have backed the canal to outlast the railway as it has done.

former milk depot — **Lord Talbot's Wharf** — well — 70' — 26 — 25 — mp — 27 — 28 — **High Onn** — Joan Eaton's Cross — Royal Oak — 29 — 30 — mp — 31 — 32 — Chamberlain's Covert — Cowley Tunnel No.33 — **Gnosall Heath** — Boat — A518 from Newport — mp — 34 — 35 — 35A — 36 — Navigation — *former flour mill* — *Millennium Way (Course of Stafford - Shrewsbury railway)* — 37 — mp — 5 — stop gate — 3

Gnosall

This appendage of Gnosall (No-zull) grew up with the coming of the canal. Two pubs slaked the thirst of passing boatmen, a steam powered flour mill took advantage of the new transport mode, and a non-conformist chapel kept a sense of proportion amidst all the excitement. Nowadays the pubs pander to pleasure boaters and passing motorists and the flour mill and chapel have become private residences.

Eating & Drinking

THE BOAT - Bridge 34. Marston's/Banks's pub with attractive curved wall abutting the bridge. Food available and pleasant garden by the water's edge. Tel: 01785 822208 - ST20 0DA

THE NAVIGATION - Bridge 35. Nice garden with good children's playground. Tel: 01785 822327 - ST20 0BN.

Fish & chips on A518 open daily (except Sundays), both sessions. Tel: 01785 822806.

Shopping

General store (with cash point) and butcher by Bridge 34.

Connections

BUSES - Arriva services to/from Stafford and Newport. Tel: 0871 200 2233.

A MASK of tall trees disguises the immensity of Shelmore embankment. It was six years in the making and, in its way, was as glorious an engineering feat as any of Telford's more visibly imposing aqueducts. A vast army of navvies and horses was employed on it. Spoil from the big cuttings at nearby Gnosall and Grub Street was brought by wagon for its construction. To Telford's dismay the earthworks slipped time after time and, as the rest of the canal was finished, Shelmore stubbornly refused to hold. In poor health, Telford struggled to oversee its completion, conscious that the bank need not have been tackled at all, had Lord Anson of Norbury Park sanctioned the preferred course through Shelmore Wood. Sadly, Norbury is no longer a junction, though the name lives on. How nice it would be to lock down the 'Seventeen Steps' of the Newport Branch and head across the marshy emptiness of Shropshire's Weald Moors to Shrewsbury. The Shrewsbury & Newport Canals Trust was formed in 2000 to campaign for restoration.

North of Norbury lies Grub Street cutting. For over a mile the canal is wrapped in a thick coat of vegetation, again, like Shelmore, hiding the sheer size of the eighty foot deep cutting, whose most unusual feature is the double-arched bridge which carries the A519 across the canal. The tiny telegraph pole is a survivor from the line which once marched beside the Shroppie for much of its length. Ironically, canals are again being used as lines of communication with the burying of optical fibres beneath selected lengths of towpath. It is to be hoped that this hi-tech activity meets with the approval of the black, monkey-like creature reputed to have haunted Bridge 39 ever since a boatman was killed here in the 19th century. Grub Street Cutting has had its towpath upgraded: thankfully, it is no longer necessary to equip yourself with a pair of fisherman's waders to negotiate it. High Offley's church sits prettily on its hillside.

Norbury Junction

An atmospheric canal community, and although the suffix is misleading nowadays, Norbury remains a busy canal centre where British Waterways have a maintenance yard. Some of the houses are still occupied by canal workers.

Eating & Drinking
JUNCTION INN - canalside Bridge 38. Tel: 01785 284288. Busy pub popular with boaters and motorists alike. Garden with children's play area. Bar and restaurant meals. ST20 0PN

ANCHOR INN - canalside Bridge 42. Tel: 01785 284569. Famously unspoilt boatman's pub serving Devizes-brewed Wadworth 6X from the jug. Gift shop to rear selling souvenirs and T-shirts. ST20 0NG.

OLD WHARF TEA ROOMS - canalside Bridge 38.

All-day, all year licensed cafe; sizeable portions of homely cooking. Tel: 01785 284292. B&B and s/c accommodation also available. ST20 0PN

Shopping
Boatyard shop: provisions, off-licence, gifts, chandlery and a wide choice of canal books.

CROSSING the border between Staffordshire and Shropshire, the canal continues to traverse an uncluttered countryside almost entirely given over to agriculture. A new crop conspicuous in neighbouring fields is elephant grass. It can come as a surprise to find so remote a landscape in the 'crowded' middle of England. One is tempted to categorise the area as 'lost' but for the obvious truth that it has never been 'found' in the first place.

Blithely we pleasure boaters sail across embankments and through cuttings with no more thought for their construction than if we were driving down the M6. But imagine the impact of Telford's brash new canal on the surrounding early nineteenth century landscape. Put yourself in the position of Sir Richard Whitworth's tenant farmer at Batchacre Park. Up until 1830 dawn rose across the open pasturelands throwing light through his east-facing windows. A year later his view of the rising sun was cut off forever by an embankment twice the height of the farmhouse. No wonder the landowners of this rural corner of Staffordshire had their misgivings, and the canal company paid dearly in compensation for the land they acquired.

West of the canal, there are good views of The Wrekin, with the Clee and Breidden hills prominent on the far horizon. It comes as something of a surprise to encounter a factory in the midst of otherwise empty countryside. It was opened by Cadbury, the chocolate manufacturers, in 1911 as a centre for processing milk collected from the dairy farming hinterland of the Shropshire Union Canal. Canal transport was used exclusively to bring countless churns gathered from numerous wharves along the canal; from simple wooden stages at the foot of fields, to the sophistication of Cadbury's own plant at High Onn. Cadbury owned a distinctive fleet of narrowboats, being one of the first operators to experiment with motorised craft. Cocoa and sugar crumb were also brought by boat to Knighton and blended with milk to make raw chocolate, itself returned to Bournville, again by boat, to be transformed into the finished delicacy. The last boatman to trade to Knighton was Charlie Atkins senior; nicknamed 'Chocolate Charlie' for obvious reasons. He carried the final cargo from Knighton to Bournville in 1961. Since then, sadly, all transport to and from the busy works has been by road. Recent rationalisation of Premier Foods has seen extra product lines centred on Knighton - now they even make Birds Custard here!

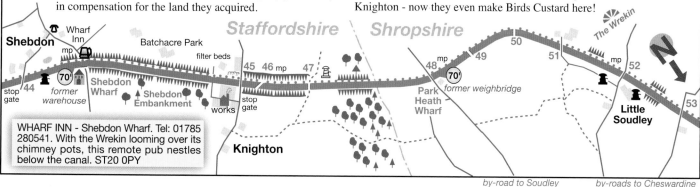

WHARF INN - Shebdon Wharf. Tel: 01785 280541. With the Wrekin looming over its chimney pots, this remote pub nestles below the canal. ST20 0PY

THE Shroppie flirts with the county boundary, the towpath forming the demarcation so that, technically, the canal lies briefly in Staffordshire. The landscape, though, is impervious to the machinations of local government, remaining aloof and typically remote: a tall, dark, silent canal, this Shropshire Union.

Woodseaves is another prodigious cutting. The canal narrows and, in places, is cut through solid rock. These cuttings proved just as troublesome to Telford and his contractors as did the embankments. There were frequent avalanches during construction and, even today, brittle lumps of sandstone are inclined to dislodge themselves and tumble into the canal; one reason why a 2mph speed limit is imposed. Well-shod and dogged walkers will be grateful for the cool shade on hot days - cyclists might find the going all but impossible: though improvements are, reputedly, in the pipeline. A feature of Woodseaves is its pair of high bridges, spanning the canal like portals to the mysterious chasms of another world. In a poem called *Don't Forget the Woodseaves Giants*, Rod Dungate (better known as a playwright) likens them to cathedral vaults, and suggests that in Woodseaves Cutting, 'time seems stripped of its power'.

At Tyrley (pronounced 'Turley') a flight of five locks - the last to be faced southbound for seventeen miles - carries the canal down into, or up out of, Market Drayton. The lower chambers are located in a shadowy sandstone cutting across which branches intertwine to form a tunnel of trees. Damp and rarely touched by sunlight, all manner of mosses and ferns flourish in this conducive environment. After dusk bats leave their tree bole roosts to hunt for insects, acrobatically twisting and turning over the luminous pounds between the locks.

Tyrley Wharf was a point of discharge and collection for the local estate at Peatswood; Cadburys also used to collect milk from here and take it by boat to their works at Knighton. The buildings date from 1837 and were erected in a graceful Tudor style by the local landowner. Nowadays, its commercial significance a thing of the dim and distant past, it would be difficult to imagine a more picturesque scene though it is sad that the craft shop and home-baking outlet, admirable enterprises of the 1980s, have both been and gone.

Summary of Facilities
Remote from any village, THE WHARF TAVERN by Bridge 55 is a popular port of call throughout the boating season and features a spacious canalside garden. Tel: 01630 661226 - TF9 2LP. Ten minutes west of Tyrley Wharf (past Tyrley's reticent little redbrick church) you'll come upon THE FOUR ALLS which offers bar and restaurant meals and also accommodation Tel: 01630 652995 - TF9 2AG

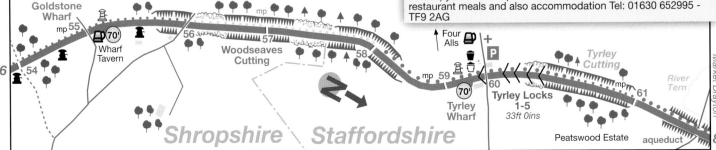

MARKET DRAYTON was the largest, in fact the *only*, town encountered by the old Birmingham & Liverpool Junction Canal on its route from Autherley to Nantwich. Naturally, a sizeable wharf was provided for dealing with local cargoes; though the canal's monopoly on local trade lasted only thirty years before the railway reached the town. It is sometimes difficult, in these days of the ubiquitous juggernaut, to appreciate the importance of the canal wharf and the railway goods yard to the past prosperity of small towns like Drayton. They must have been the hub of local life, few businesses would have been able to carry out their trade without regular recourse to the wharfinger and the stationmaster. From the opening of the canal until the First World War no commodity, apart from local agricultural produce, could have arrived at Market Drayton, or been dispatched, without the involvement of these important gentlemen. On the canal a large basin and a sizeable warehouse and adjoining cornmill remind us of this lost significance.

Pleasant 48 hour moorings, bordered by school playing fields, stretch south from Bridge 62 to the imposing aqueduct over the lane to Peatswood - Map 7. Steps lead down to the road below, which crosses the little River Tern nearby and forms the most romantic, but not perhaps the most convenient, approach to the town centre.

The canal makes a quick getaway north of Drayton. By Bridge 65, H. Orwell & Son have added boatyard facilities to their traditional business as coal merchants. Note the substantial stone abutments where the North Staffordshire Railway once crossed the canal. Another long lost railway accompanies the canal past Adderley.

Betton Cutting is not among 'The Shroppie's' most dramatic, but it is reputed to be haunted by a shrieking spectre, and working boatmen would avoid lingering here in the old days. Indeed, it could be said that this whole canal has something of a fey quality about it, a blurring of past and present which is liable to send shivers down susceptible spines. The last time we tried to walk through the cutting it looked as if the towpath had been annexed by grazing cattle!

The Adderley flight is neat and tidy, although not the place it was under Frank Butter's care thirty years ago when every chamber was bordered by flower beds and the grass manicured like a bowling green. A privet hedge beside the third lock down indicates the site of a demolished lock-keeper's cottage, one of many to have disappeared from the canal system over the years. Adderley's distant and distinctly classical church is worth a pilgrimage, much of it being in the care of the Churches Conservation Trust. Keys are available locally.

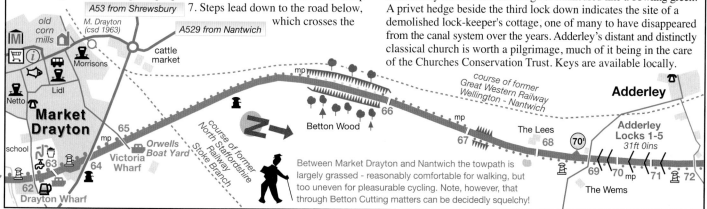

old corn mills

M. Drayton (csd 1963)

A53 from Shrewsbury

A529 from Nantwich

Morrisons

cattle market

Lidl

Netto

Market Drayton

65

mp

Orwells Boat Yard

Victoria Wharf

course of former North Staffordshire Railway Stoke Branch

school

63

64

62

Drayton Wharf

A53 to The Potteries

mp

Betton Wood

66

67

68

course of former Great Western Railway Wellington - Nantwich

mp

The Lees

70'

Adderley

Adderley Locks 1-5
31ft 0ins

69 70 mp 71 72

9

7

The Wems

Between Market Drayton and Nantwich the towpath is largely grassed - reasonably comfortable for walking, but too uneven for pleasurable cycling. Note, however, that through Betton Cutting matters can be decidedly squelchy!

Talbot Wharf, Holidays Afloat, Betton Wharf   *for details of facilities at Market Drayton turn to page 18*

Market Drayton

Map 8

The conspicuous Second World War pillbox guarding Bridge 62 is not, despite first impressions, still in situ as a deterrent to visitors. Self-styled as 'The Home of Gingerbread', Drayton is best visited on a Wednesday when the ancient market is in full swing and country folk gather to seek out a bargain and a gossip. This is the town's real heritage, along with its half-timbered houses which mostly date from the aftermath of a fire that swept through the place in 1651. Drayton's most famous son was Robert Clive, best remembered here for scaling the sturdy tower of St Mary's and for blackmailing local shopkeepers - ideal escapades in preparation for a career in diplomacy and military leadership. He established British rule in the Sub Continent and became known as 'Clive of India'. Betjeman and Piper's Shell Guide of 1951 recalls that the district was once terrorised by a murderous gang known as 'The Bravoes of Market Drayton'. On Saturday nights, as the pubs empty, it's easy to believe they are still at large. To the west of the town lie the large premises of Muller - 'the UK's most loved dairy product brand' - whilst on the northern fringe is Drayton's Livestock Market, a flourishing centre for agricultural buying and selling; at times excitable bidding can be heard, borne on the wind as far out as the towpath.

Eating & Drinking

THE TALBOT - adjacent Bridge 62. Tel: 01630 654989. A handsome, red brick Georgian inn just east of the canal. TF9 1HW

STAFFORD COURT HOTEL - Stafford Street. Tel: 01630 652646. Bar & restaurant food in small, but well-appointed town centre hotel. TF9 1HY

THE BUTTERCROSS - town centre tea room. Tel: 01630 656250. Coffees & teas, oatcakes & omelettes. TF9 1PF

Shopping

It was sobering to see so many boarded-up shops on our most recent research trip. It can't be easy for small market towns to compete these days, let alone small independent shops. Yet Market Drayton tries hard and looks its best on a Wednesday, market day. WILLIAMS OF WEM is a fine delicatessen beside the handsome Buttercross. Branches of all the main banks, a post office, launderette (though quite a hike from the canal - ask at the TIC for directions!) and Lidl, Morrisons, and Netto supermarkets will cater adequately for most boaters' requirements.

Things to Do

TOURIST INFORMATION - Cheshire Street. Tel:01630 653114 www.marketdrayton.gov.uk TF9 1PH MUSEUM - Shropshire Street. Tel: 01630 657455. Open Wednesdays, Saturdays and Sunday (afternoons) from April to October. Admission free. Local history nostalgically displayed in an old shop. TF9 3DA

Connections

BUSES - X64 services hourly Mon-Sat, bi-hourly Sun to/from Stoke and Shrewsbury. Tel: 0871 200 2233.

TAXIS - First Call Taxis. Tel: 01630 653200.

Tyrley Wharf

Karen Tanguy

FIFTEEN locks running through a cutting of larch and Scots pine take the canal across the Shropshire/Cheshire border. The locks are well-maintained and a pleasure to operate. Vegetables and fruit are often available from an honesty box by Lock 9. The barrel-roofed building by Lock 10 was used by stonemasons, blacksmiths and carpenters engaged in maintaining the flight. Towards the foot of the flight - known to old boatmen as the Audlem "Thick" - you pass Audlem Wharf, one of the prettiest ports of call on the Shropshire Union, with a former warehouse restored as a popular pub and the adjacent lofty mill converted into a superb craft shop.

North of the bottom lock, below which is a well preserved stable block used as a base by the Daystar Theatre Group, the canal, wide with concrete banking but deceptively shallow, bounds across the infant River Weaver on a high embankment. One of the crazier notions of the Ministry of War Transport during the Second World War was to make the Weaver navigable by 100 ton barges to this point, beyond which a lift would carry them up to the level of the Shropshire Union, upgraded sufficiently for them to travel as far south as Wolverhampton. Bridge 80 retains its early British Waterways era blue and yellow number plate, immediately to the south, a drainage paddle is embossed 'SUC Ellesmere 1928'; twin artefacts of enduring value.

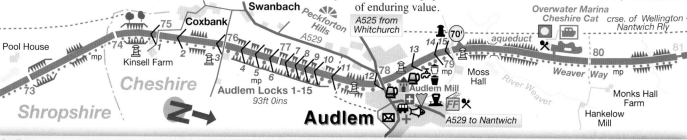

Audlem

"The sleepers sleep at Audlem" sang Flanders and Swann in *Slow Train*, their elegy for the Beeching cuts, and whilst they were referring to the village's station and its imminent closure, Audlem remains a sleepy sort of place. Now that the trains have gone and the average motorist is hell bent on getting somewhere else fast, only the canal traveller is journeying at a pace to do justice to this lovely village, highpoints of which are the ancient buttermarket and parish church.

Eating & Drinking

THE BRIDGE - canalside Bridge 78. Tel: 01270 811267. Marstons, food. Sunday carvery, WIFI. CW3 0DX

THE SHROPPIE FLY - canalside Lock 13. Tel: 01270 811772. Nicely furnished warehouse conversion serving bar and restaurant meals. CW3 0DX

THE LORD COMBERMERE - The Square. Tel: 01270 812277. Refurbished village centre pub. CW3 0AQ

JUST THE PLAICE TOO - Cheshire Street. Fish & chips. Tel: 01270 812242. CW3 0AH

OLD PRIESTS HOUSE - The Square. All day breakfasts, coffees, teas and light lunches. Tel: 01270 811749. CW3 0AH

KEBABLAND - Tel: 01270 812226. Take-away.

Connections

BUSES - services to/from Nantwich and Whitchurch Mon-Sat. Tel: 0871 200 2233.

Shopping

Shopping here a pleasure rather than a stressful chore. Fresh to this reprint are a health food outlet (Hoc's Fat Pigeon) and bicycle shop. Cash machine at the Co-op. Laundry facilities at the new Overwater Marina adjacent Bridge 80. AUDLEM MILL CANAL SHOP - Tel: 01270 811059. Christine and Peter Silvester have taken over the mantle of John Stothert with aplomb and this handsome waterside mill continues to be one of the best canal shops on the system. Additional emphasis now on needlework and crafts for which courses are offered. www.audlemmill.co.uk CW3 0DX

Audlem

AT Hack Green there are two isolated locks and the remnants of a stable, recalling the practice of frequent changing of horses on the 'fly' boats which travelled day and night with urgent, perishable cargoes. This is the Cheshire Plain and dairy farming has long been a vital part of the area's economy - though for how much longer one might wonder, given the precarious state of agriculture at the beginning of the 21st century. One option might be to replace cows with canal boats! On the occasion of our most recent research trip, locals were debating whether plans for a new marina - on farmland to the north of the Weaver aqueduct - would be good for Audlem or otherwise. Another new initiative affecting the canal is the adoption of its towpath as part of the Weaver Way - though it seems a decade may elapse before the scheme is fully completed. For some boggy sections of towpath it can't come soon enough!

When we first explored this canal in the early Eighties we were blissfully unaware of Hack Green's nuclear bunker, a Second World War radar station secretly designated to play a role as a Regional Government Headquarters in the event of a nuclear war. Deemed redundant at the end of the Cold War, it has somewhat bizarrely become a tourist attraction.

Adroitly changing the subject, let us recall how trade survived on this canal until the 1960s; which must be some sort of testimony to the viability of canal carrying. Perhaps in the final analysis attitudes rather than economics prevailed. One of the most celebrated traffics on the Shroppie in latter years was Thomas Clayton's oil run from Stanlow on the banks of the Mersey to Langley Green, near Oldbury in the Black Country. The contract commenced in 1924 and the Clayton boats, with their characteristic decked holds, and river names, were a mainstay of trade on the canal for thirty years. Even post-war, a thousand boat-loads per annum were being despatched from Stanlow, some remaining horse-drawn until the early Fifties. But, in common with other canals, the Shropshire Union lost its final freights to the motor lorry; then, for many, with the disappearance of its working boats, something died on the Shroppie, some intangible component of canal heritage that no amount of preservation, nor hectic holiday trade, can ever quite compensate for.

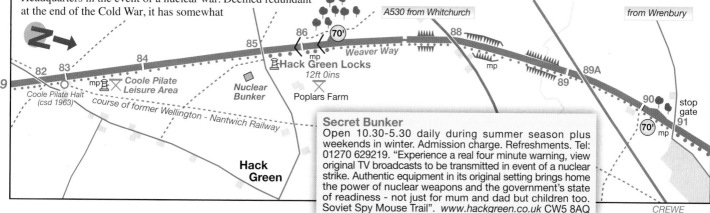

Secret Bunker
Open 10.30-5.30 daily during summer season plus weekends in winter. Admission charge. Refreshments. Tel: 01270 629219. "Experience a real four minute warning, view original TV broadcasts to be transmitted in event of a nuclear strike. Authentic equipment in its original setting brings home the power of nuclear weapons and the government's state of readiness - not just for mum and dad but children too. Soviet Spy Mouse Trail". www.hackgreen.co.uk CW5 8AQ

11 SHROPSHIRE UNION CANAL

THE character of the Shropshire Union Canal changes perceptibly at Nantwich: northwards lie the broad, winding waters of its earlier constituent, the Chester Canal, opened in 1779; southwards the direct and narrow Birmingham & Liverpool Junction Canal, upon which work began here in 1827, though five years elapsed before the embankment settled sufficiently for the canal to be opened. Northbound, it's easy to feel lost without the reassuringly regular appearance of those elegant mileposts which have accompanied you from Autherley.

Long before the advent of the canals, Nantwich was reduced to ashes by the Great Fire of 1583 which lasted for almost three weeks. Four bears, thoughtfully released for their own safety, are said to have 'considerably hampered' attempts to douse the flames! Concerned for the area's salt industry, Queen Elizabeth donated a thousand pounds towards the town's rebuilding fund. Sixty years later Nantwich sided with the Parliamentarians during the Civil War, the only Cheshire town to do so. In 1644 its citizens were besieged by the Royalists for six weeks. An annual re-enactment celebrates their relief on the 25th January.

The broad embankment elevates the canal above the housing, back gardens and allotments which constitute the periphery of Nantwich. Ironically, these earthworks, together with a cast iron aqueduct over the Chester road, could have been avoided if the owners of Dorfold Hall had not objected to the passage of the canal across their land. A Sculpture Trail has been laid out beside the embankment's refurbished towpath, the main exhibit being in the form of a boat horse built out of reclaimed lockgates. Visitor moorings are provided along the length of the embankment, and they make for a pleasant overnight stay with easy access to the town centre, an enjoyable ten minutes stroll to the east.

The basin and former terminus of the Chester Canal, hints at the more expedient route to the south which Telford would have liked to have used. Nowadays it's pretty choc-a-bloc with boats, but there's a certain pleasure to be had from manoeuvring in and out of its narrow confines to get a pump-out or fill up with diesel: all a far cry from 1939 when Tom and Angela Rolt couldn't get *Cressy* into the basin because a bar of silt, built up by the passage of motor boats, prevented their entry. Adjoining the basin are the premises of the Nantwich & Border Counties Yachting Club, an organisation whose founder members were early advocates of the use of the canal system for leisure.

Between Nantwich and Hurleston Junction (Map 12) the former Chester Canal passes uneventfully through a landscape typical of the Cheshire Plain.

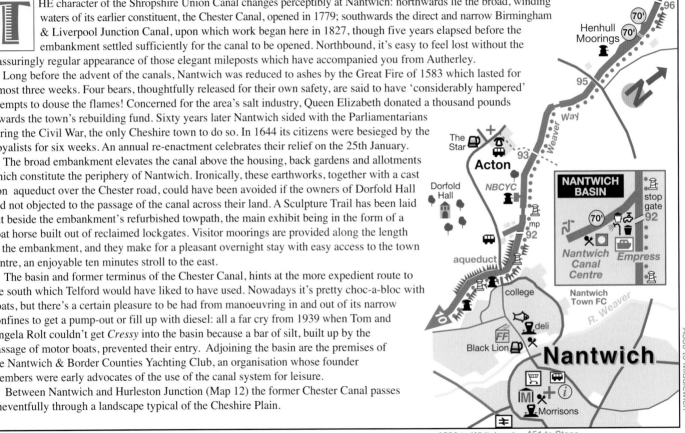

North or south, there are few English towns of this size nicer than Nantwich. The octagonal tower of St Mary's church, glimpsed across freshly-built rooftops from the high canal embankment, tempts you to moor and get to know this picturesque and historic Cheshire town. Walking in from the basin, the aqueduct forms an appropriate portcullis, and the appeal of the town increases as the centre is reached. Welsh Row is a handsome thoroughfare: keep your eyes peeled for the Tollemache Almshouses, Cheshire Constabulary police houses, Primitive Methodist chapel and Town Well House (No.52). In medieval times Nantwich was the chief salt producing town in the county. Elizabeth, wife of John Milton, of *Paradise Lost* fame, was buried in the grounds of the town's first Baptist Chapel in 1727. For a brief Victorian heyday Nantwich flourished as a spa town. On closer inspection, there are bullet holes in the fabric of the church, where traitors and spies were executed by firing squad during the Civil War. Inside the medieval wood carving is magnificent.

Eating & Drinking
BLACK LION - Welsh Row. Tel: 01270 628711. *Good Beer Guide* recommended 17th century half-timbered pub on way into town. Weetwood ales from nearby Tarporley. CW5 5ED

CURSHAWS - Welsh Row. Tel: 01270 623020. Stylish modern eaterie on way into town. CW5 5ED

ROMAZZINO - Love Lane (off Pillory Street). Tel: 01270 626456. Well appointed Italian open for lunch and dinner daily. CW5 5BH

AUSTINS - Hospital Street. Tel: 01270 625491. Consciously old fashioned coffee house which transcends kitsch by virtue of its range of comfort food including their very own bangers and mash, cottage pie, omelettes, cakes. Open Tue, Thur, Fri & Sat 10am to 3.30pm; Wed 10am to noon. CW5 5RL

CAFE DE PARIS - Hospital Street. Tel: 01270 620180. Charming oasis of an establishment run, not by a Parisian, but by a gentleman from Orleans. Coffees, soups, baguettes, French pastries and light lunches. CW5 5RP

NATRAJ - Tel: 01270 620600. Indian restaurant housed in former booking hall of railway station. CW5 5YR

If you're making the mistake of not going into town, there's a nice little cafe at Nantwich Canal Centre.

Shopping
More affluent than Market Drayton, Nantwich's antique shops and boutiques emphasise its position at the centre of a Gucci-heeled hinterland. Keep a tight rein on your womenfolk - without firm male guidance they will run amok in Nantwich's fine clothes, shoes, and household goods outlets. But it is perhaps the food sellers that are most satisfying: butchers like CLEWLOWS (try their pea and ham pies!), bakers like CHATWINS (whose headquarters are in the town) and fishmongers like SEA BREEZES all of whom have outlets in Pepper Street. NANTWICH BOOKSHOP overlooks the Town Square and is an excellent independent with a pavement cafe and/or coffee lounge where you can dip into any newly acquired reading matter. On Hospital Street are EDENCROFT wines and BROOKSHAWS butchers. A bit further along, on the opposite side, are A. T. WELCH's surprisingly narrow yet deep premises housing butcher, grocer, delicatessen and coffee merchant counters which reinvent themselves, at the far end, into Austins retro coffee shop - see Eating & Drinking.

The indoor market hall is open on Tuesdays, Thursdays and Saturdays, and features an eclectic range of stalls. There are MORRISONS and ALDI supermarkets whilst A. F. CYCLES offer repairs from their premises on Welsh Row - Tel: 01270 628870. Excellent laundry facilities are available at the canal basin.

Things to Do
TOURIST INFORMATION - Civic Hall. Tel: 01270 610983. *www.crewe-nantwich.gov.uk*

NANTWICH MUSEUM - Pillory Street. Tel: 01270 627104. Well presented displays of local history. Free admission. CW5 5BQ

Connections
BUSES - Arriva service 84 connects quarter-hourly Mon-Sat and hourly Sun with Crewe (though not directly with the railway station) in one direction and Chester in the other with useful stops at Barbridge and Calveley for towpath walkers. Tel: 0871 200 2233.

TRAINS - services to/from Crewe and Shrewsbury via Wrenbury and Whitchurch. Tel: 08457 484950.

TAXIS - Direct. Tel: 01270 585000.

A short walk across the fields from Bridge 93 leads to this village which at first seems to consist mainly of former council houses. The imposing church however repays investigation, and amongst the gravestones you'll come upon that of A. N. Hornby, the English cricket captain whose one-off defeat to Australia at The Oval in 1882 brought about a spoof obituary which referred to the cremated 'remains' of the English game being sent to Australia, hence the origin of 'The Ashes'.

THE STAR - Tel: 01270 627296. 17th century half-timbered inn mentioned in *Narrow Boat*. CW5 8LD

HURLESTON and Barbridge are the 'Clapham Junctions' of the inland waterways. During the cruising season the section between them is often frenetic with boats converging and diverging to and from all points of the canal compass. Fortunately, the old Chester Canal was built to barge dimensions and there is plenty of room to manoeuvre. The Cheshire Plain's recurring image of spacious pastures grazed by Friesian cattle continues unabated.

Remote and frequently windswept, the Middlewich Branch of the Shropshire Union cuts across the grain of the landscape on a series of high embankments. It can be a busy length of canal for, as well as funnelling boats to and from the Llangollen Canal, it is also an integral component of the popular Four Counties Ring. There are four locks on the Middlewich; deep and heavy gated, they can become bottlenecks at the beginning and end of the week in high summer. Two marinas add to the hustle and bustle.

Map labels

13
103
102
pinfold
Wardle
Barbridge Junction
101
Jolly Tar
narrows at site of former warehouse
Olde Barbridge Inn
1
2
3
4
Barbridge Marina & Midway Boats
100
CHESTER
99
70'
Cholmondeston Lock
11ft 3ins
Venetian Marine
5
5A
CREWE
98
pipe
reservoir
Llangollen Canal
18
Hurleston Junction
97
Hurleston Locks
34ft 3ins
A51 to Nantwich
11
6
70'
Weaver Way
Minshull Lock
11ft 0ins
B5074 from Winsford
Middlewich Branch
7
8
9
28
Aqueduct Marina
B5074 to Nantwich

Barbridge

Barbridge Junction is an amazingly popular overnight mooring spot, and it pays to get here early at the height of the season to be sure of a place. Main road apart, it's easy to see its attraction, with two pubs vying for custom and the interest of the junction itself, where a transhipment shed once spanned the main line. You can detect its site where the canal narrows just south of the junction. How about a Lottery-funded rebuild?

Eating & Drinking

OLDE BARBRIDGE INN - Bridge 100. Tel: 01270 528443. CW5 6AY
JOLLY TAR - opposite the junction. Tel: 01270 528283. CW5 6BE
There are cafes on the Middlewich Branch at both Venetian Marine and Aqueduct Marina.

Connections

BUSES - Arriva service 84 links Chester with Crewe via Nantwich quarter hourly Mon-Sat and hourly Sun. Tel: 0871 200 2233.

*Figures refer to main line - allow 1.5hrs for this section of the Middlewich Branch

THIS is an intoxicating length of waterway, full of contrasts in landscape: the wooded defile at Tilstone Bank; the glorious line of close-cropped hills running north of the two Beeston locks; and most dramatic of all for travellers heading northwards, the first detailed glimpses of Beeston Castle, over five hundred feet high on its lonely outcrop. Through all this the little River Gowy chuckles to its Mersey outfall, draining the rolling farmland. But, scintillating scenery apart, it bears remembering that the old Chester Canal had a living to earn, and throughout this section there are well preserved examples of former commerce, notably the former transhipment wharf between canal and railway at Calveley, now under the aegis of British Waterways as a 'Service Station'.

Bunbury is a fascinating canal environment. The widebeam staircase locks make an obvious centrepiece. Alongside them is a fine stable block, recalling the practice of exchanging fresh horses for tired ones on the fast 'fly boats' which covered the 80 miles between the Mersey ports and the Black Country factories in just over 24 hours. These premises are now occupied by Anglo Welsh, their offices and shop being accommodated in an adjacent warehouse still displaying the faded legend 'Shropshire Union Railways & Canal Co' on its north facing gable end.

Tilstone Lock lies in a gorgeous setting. Beside it a mill stands astride the Gowy, dating from 1838 and restored

for residential use. A curious circular building overlooks the head of the lock chamber. There are others at Beeston and Tarvin locks and they were once used by lengthsmen to store maintenance equipment. Beneath a sweeping ridge reminiscent of the South Downs stand the two Beeston locks: the upper built conventionally of stone, the lower unusually of iron plates - Telford's way of dealing with ground instability at this point; it is not advisable to attempt fitting two narrow boats side by side in this lock. Beeston Castle Wharf never fails to entertain: the auction mart is well worth investigating; deer now graze on the hillside which conceals Second World War oil storage tanks; and a charming old signal box perches on the railway embankment, still bearing the closed station's appellation - Beeston Castle & Tarporley.

Summary of Facilities

THE DAVENPORT ARMS - Bridge 104. Tel: 01829 262684. Pub reinvigorated after facing closure. Good menu. CW6 9JN

BUNBURY MILL - half a mile south west of Bridge 105. Tel: 01829 261422. Charmingly restored water mill beside the Gowy. Open Sunday and Bank Holiday afternoons between April and Sep. Souvenirs and flour for sale. CW6 9PP

BEESTON CASTLE HOTEL - Bridge 107. Tel: 01829 260234. Popular pub/restaurant also offering accommodation. CW6 9NJ

RINGSIDE CAFE - Bridge 107. Eavesdrop on auction ring gossip.

LOCK GATE CAFE - Bridge 107. Open daily for breakfasts, lunches and teas. *Anglo Welsh also have a cafe at their Bunbury boatyard.*

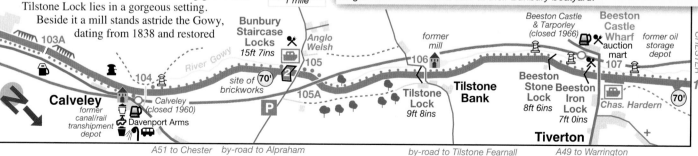

BEESTON Castle dominates the landscape, like a visitor from another planet, an upturned plum pudding of an outcrop, a geological afterthought commandeered by Medieval man for a fortress. Behind it the Peckforton Hills ride the horizon like surfers on an Atlantic beach. This is good hiking country. The Sandstone Trail, a 34 mile footpath across Cheshire's backbone from Frodsham to Whitchurch, crosses the canal at Wharton's Lock and may be conveniently linked with the towpath and other public footpaths to form a number of circular walks.

Bate's Mill survives as an enviable private residence. A country road swoops down to cross the millstream and an adjacent expanse of water is the haunt of wildfowl. Nearby, the canal is carried over the Gowy on an embankment framed with conifers. Trains thread their way through the fields in the middle distance, but otherwise the world seems undisturbed. In the long pound between Wharton's and Christleton locks the boater has plenty of time for peaceful reflection and communion with nature. A large new marina adds considerably to boat movements in the vicinity.

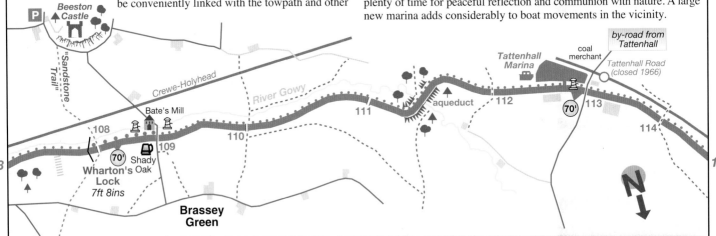

Tilstone Lock

ALTHOUGH the countryside is conspicuously flat, the Peckforton Hills to the south and Delamere Forest to the north-east give your gaze something to linger over; whilst, if the elements have blessed you with a clear day, the brooding summits of Celtic Wales are to be discerned on the western rim of the world. Long lines of moored craft make the responsible boater's progress irritatingly slow in the vicinity of Hargrave. Smart boats, sad boats, new boats, neglected boats echo their absent owners' character and commitment; even some of the names mock at aspirations unachieved. As they approach Bridge 115, motorists honk their horns like Mediterraneans.

Probably the very earliest hire cruisers on the canal system were available from a boatyard at Christleton which began hiring to intrepid holidaymakers way back in 1935. In those days you could hire a small cruiser for £4 a week, though you also had to fork out ten shillings in tolls to the LMS Railway who owned the canal prior to Nationalisation in 1947.

In the late Twenties, a Chester man, T. W. Cubbon, wrote an account (*Only a Little Cockboat*) of a voyage, in a canvas covered boat powered by a petrol engine, from Chester along the Shropshire Union and Staffs & Worcs canals to the rivers Severn and Avon. In the book he relates his first night on the canal at Egg Bridge moored abreast a widebeam barge, but being forced to move on in the small hours of the morning because rats from the barge had boarded his boat! The barges and the rats may have gone, but signs of former commerce remain at Egg Bridge and Christleton in the form of handsome canalside mills. At Christleton the canal commences its descent to Chester and the surface of the towpath improves, being laudably well-maintained all the way from here to Ellesmere Port.

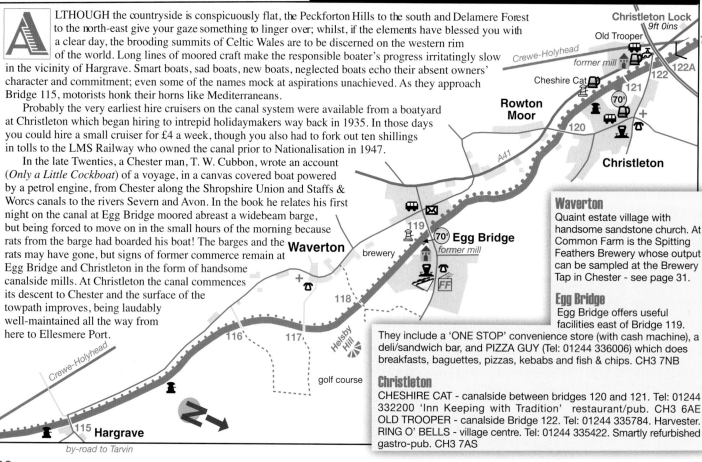

Waverton
Quaint estate village with handsome sandstone church. At Common Farm is the Spitting Feathers Brewery whose output can be sampled at the Brewery Tap in Chester - see page 31.

Egg Bridge
Egg Bridge offers useful facilities east of Bridge 119. They include a 'ONE STOP' convenience store (with cash machine), a deli/sandwich bar, and PIZZA GUY (Tel: 01244 336006) which does breakfasts, baguettes, pizzas, kebabs and fish & chips. CH3 7NB

Christleton
CHESHIRE CAT - canalside between bridges 120 and 121. Tel: 01244 332200 'Inn Keeping with Tradition' restaurant/pub. CH3 6AE
OLD TROOPER - canalside Bridge 122. Tel: 01244 335784. Harvester.
RING O' BELLS - village centre. Tel: 01244 335422. Smartly refurbished gastro-pub. CH3 7AS

THE canal traveller's approach to the centre of Chester is overtly suburban and industrial, characteristics which belie the grace and romance of the city within its walls. Frankly, you could be forgiven for thinking that a Blackburn or a Burnley lay immediately ahead and it is with some relief that the centre is reached and the Chester of the tourist propaganda manifests itself. Yet even workaday Chester has its highlights: the Victorian waterworks below Chemistry Lock: the lead shot tower originally used for making musket shot during the Napoleonic Wars: and gaunt warehouses (now converted into flats and pubs and clubs) which overlook the canal as it passes through an area of the city once vital to the coffers of the Shropshire Union. Widebeam barges known as Mersey 'flats' traded down from Ellesmere Port to Chester and, less often, southwards to Barbridge and Nantwich.

West of the centre lies Tower Wharf and the short Dee Branch linking the canal with the river. The canalscape here is full of interest: Telford's warehouse with its arched loading bay; an elegant canopied drydock; a large boatbuilding yard where the Shropshire Union carrying fleet was once built and maintained; and the rare fascination of two adjacent canal levels.

Tower Wharf 2

Tower Wharf 1

The former North Basin - thoughtlessly infilled in the Fifties - has been re-dug and re-watered as part of a redevelopment scheme. A plaque on Bridge 126 commemorates L. T. C. Rolt's championing of the canals.

But it is the canal's juxtaposition with Chester's great red medieval wall which is its most memorable gesture and image. The round tower from which King Charles I saw his Cavaliers beaten looms out over the water so dramatically that the canal resembles a defensive moat, which is exactly what it once was, and the canal builders took good advantage of this defensive channel. Not so easy was the construction of the gargantuan Northgate staircase locks which had to be hewn out of solid rock.

The Chester Canal predated the Wirral Line by a matter of twenty years or so and, originally, the link with the River Dee continued direct from the foot of Northgate Locks, which at that time consisted of five chambers. The existing layout dates from the advent of the route from Ellesmere Port and the branch down to the Dee describes a dog-leg course through three locks to meet the tidal river; a waterway not accessible other than by pre-arrangement and certainly not one for novices or the faint-hearted!

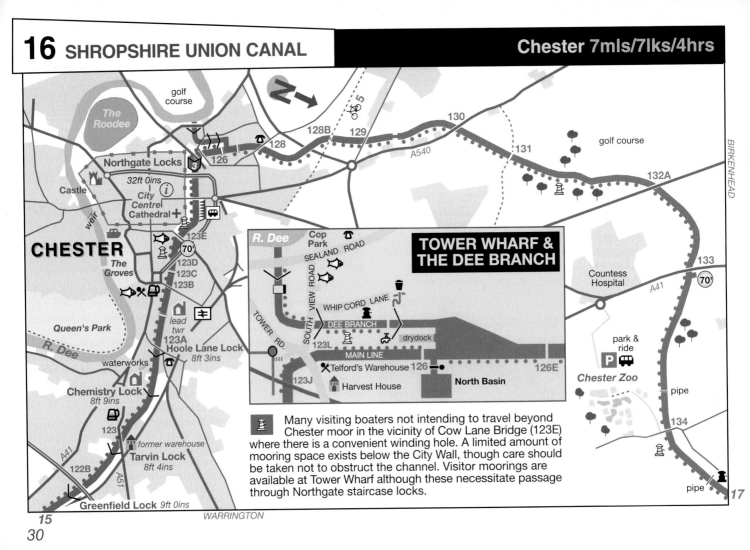

golf course

N

5

The Roodee

128B

129

130

A540

131

golf course

132A

BIRKENHEAD

Northgate Locks

3

126

128

32ft 0ins

i

Castle

City Centre Cathedral

weir

CHESTER

70'

123E

123D

133

133

Countess Hospital

A41

70'

The Groves

123C

123B

TOWER WHARF & THE DEE BRANCH

R. Dee

Cop Park

SEALAND ROAD

SOUTH VIEW ROAD

WHIP CORD LANE

DEE BRANCH

drydock

123L

MAIN LINE

123J

Telford's Warehouse 126

Harvest House

North Basin

126E

park & ride

P

Chester Zoo

Queen's Park

R. Dee

lead twr

123A

Hoole Lane Lock
8ft 3ins

waterworks

Chemistry Lock
8ft 9ins

123

former warehouse

Tarvin Lock
8ft 4ins

A41

122B

A51

Greenfield Lock *9ft 0ins*

pipe

134

pipe

17

Many visiting boaters not intending to travel beyond Chester moor in the vicinity of Cow Lane Bridge (123E) where there is a convenient winding hole. A limited amount of mooring space exists below the City Wall, though care should be taken not to obstruct the channel. Visitor moorings are available at Tower Wharf although these necessitate passage through Northgate staircase locks.

Chester

On Sunday mornings, Chester breathes like a sleeping child and footsteps echo your progress around the city wall, the perfect introduction to this lovely city. At most other times, though, shoppers and tourists transform Chester into a frenetic, free-for-all from which you are apt to go scurrying back to your boat for refuge. But in all of Britain's inland waterways, only York can vie with Chester when it comes to antiquity, and the city wall, which kept enemies at bay down the centuries, now keeps 21st century reality in its place. Once through the ancient gateways you are wrapped in a medieval time warp which makes Chester the most agreeable of places to saunter in and absorb the atmosphere.

It was the Romans who founded the city, seeing it as a likely place to build a port and keep a weather eye on the troublesome Marches; they called it Deva. In the Dark Ages the Anglo Saxons undid much of their predecessors' civilisation, but by the Middle Ages Chester was flourishing again and a 12th century writer noted ships from Aquitaine, Germany and Spain at berth in the shadow of the city wall. Chester's celebrated 'Rows' are thought to have had their origins during this period. These covered galleries above street level are quite unique, and elevate window-shopping into a pleasurable experience for all.

During the Civil War the city supported King Charles, but it did him little good for it was from the walls of Chester that he saw his army defeated on Rowton Heath. Victorian Chester grew up outside the city wall, beyond the canal and out towards the railway. What the Victorians did inside the wall is best forgotten by those romantics who like to think that all that black and white half timbering is original.

Eating & Drinking

BOLLICINI - Rufus Court, Northgate. Tel: 01244 329932. Stylish restaurant bar. CH1 2JH

TELFORD'S WAREHOUSE - Tower Wharf. Tel: 01244 390090. Eat and drink in Telford's handsome canal warehouse - what would the great man make of it? Weetwood beers from Tarporley. CH1 4EZ

OLD HARKER ARMS - Bridge 123B. Tel: 01244 344525. Well-appointed warehouse conversion. Wide range of real ales and good choice of food. Up the steps on City Road stand a plethora of ethnic restaurants. CH3 5AL

MILL HOTEL - by Bridge 123C. Tel: 01244 350035. Restaurant, bar food and a bewildering choice of real ale. Restaurant boat. CH1 3NF

THE BREWERY TAP - Lower Bridge Street. Tel: 01244 340999. Good food and locally brewed ales (plus guests) from Waverton in ancient high-ceilinged house. CH1 1RU

JOSEPH BENJAMIN - Northgate. Tel: 01244 344295. Deli tucked into the wall beneath a secondhand bookshop. Charmingly small, award-winning restaurant open daily (ex Mon) until 5pm and for dinner Thur-Sat. CH1 2HT

EGO - Grosvenor Street. Tel: 01244 346512. Reliable growing chain of Mediterranean restaurants. CH1 2DD

UNION VAULTS - Egerton Street (by Bridge 123 C). Tel: 01244 405566. *Good Beer Guide* recommended back street local . CH1 3ND

THE SLOW BOAT - Bridge 123E. Tel: 01244 317873. Asian fusion restaurant overlooking the canal. CH1 3JJ

Shopping

One of the most amenable shopping centres in Britain. THE ROWS contain some of the most up-market shops in the city within their fascinating galleries, whilst ST MICHAEL'S ARCADE is a Victorian arcade of soaring iron and glass reached off Bridge Street Row. THE FORUM is an indoor market open daily (except Sunday), where stalls specialise in fresh Cheshire produce, crafts and antiques. Don't miss THE CHEESE SHOP (Tel: 01244 346240) on Northgate.

Things to Do

TOURIST INFORMATION CENTRE - Town Hall, Northgate. Tel: 01244 402111. Accompanied walks depart daily from the TIC. CH1 2HS *www.chestertourism.com*

CHESTER CATHEDRAL - One of England's ecclesiastical masterpieces. Tel: 01244 324756. CH1 2HU *www.chestercathedral.com*

DEWA ROMAN EXPERIENCE - Pierpoint Lane. Tel: 01244 343407. Open daily 9am-5pm. Roman remains! CH1 1NL

GROSVENOR MUSEUM - Grosvenor Street. Museum of local history. Admission free, open daily. Tel: 01244 402008. CH1 2DD

CITY SIGHTSEEING - open top bus tours. Tel: 01244 347457.

CHESTER BOAT - From the boating station on The Groves aboard Bithells launches. Tel: 01244 325394. CH1 1SD

CHESTER ZOO - One of Europe's finest zoos. Admission charge, open daily. Best reached from the canal via Bridge 134. Tel: 01244 380280. CH2 1EU

Connections

BUSES - bus station on George Street off Northgate. Tel: 0871 200 2233. Service 1 runs every 20 minutes (hourly Sun) to Ellesmere Port, a 35 minute ride away. Service 84 (half-hourly Mon-Sat, hourly Sun) shadows the Shropshire Union most of the way down to Nantwich. TRAINS - railway station on City Road, reached from Bridge 123B. Tel: 08457 484950. Free bus link to city centre for rail ticket holders. TAXIS - Abbey Taxis. Tel: 01244 344344.

COMPARATIVELY few boaters reaching Chester from the south elect to continue along the Shropshire Union main line to its historic terminus on the banks of the River Mersey at Ellesmere Port. Beguiled by Chester's magnificence they languish in its spell, prisoners of the misconception that nothing worthy of their attention lies beyond Tower Wharf. In fact exploring the northern end of the Shropshire Union and stopping short at Chester is akin to not listening to the end of Beethoven's 5th Symphony, or omitting the cheese board at the Savoy.

Travelling northwards, urban Chester is soon left behind and one enters seemingly remote pastureland of no great beauty, but where peace prevails. More linear moorings slow the boater, but such delays can be redeemed as you near Ellesmere Port where a good depth of water enables the throttle to be exercised without fear of making a wash.

Dating from 1795, the canal between Chester and Ellesmere Port was part of the grandiose Ellesmere Canal scheme to link the Mersey with the Severn. Known as the Wirral line, it quickly attracted traffic; not only freight but passengers too, for a horse-drawn packet service connected Chester with Ellesmere Port where travellers could change to another boat to reach Liverpool. The passenger business flourished until the coming of the Railway Age, freight well into it. Indeed, narrowboats continued to trade from Ellesmere Port with oil for the Midlands until the mid 1950s. One of the most famous of these craft, *Gifford*, may be seen at the National Waterways Museum. Now, of course, the railway has declined also; hard to believe that boat trains once raced this way from London to connect with Atlantic liners on the Mersey. Today's more mundane transport makes an appearance

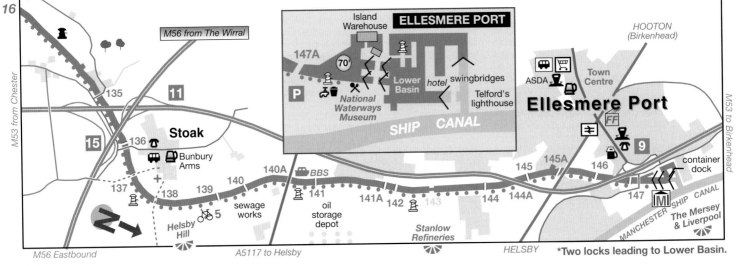

at Stoak in the shape of two motorways.

Northwards from Stoak, the gleaming refineries of Stanlow define themselves on the horizon, indicating that Ellesmere Port is near at hand. No-one would pretend, even in a guidebook, that the approach to the town is pretty, but anticipation outweighs purely aesthetic considerations, and there's a rising sense of excitement in anticipating your first sight of the Manchester Ship Canal and the wide Mersey.

A limited amount of mooring space is usually available between the motorway bridge and the museum entrance, for boaters intending to stay just a short time in the vicinity. Preferable though, in our opinion, are the spacious moorings in the lower basin reached through the locks. To access them you will have to report to the museum's reception desk and pay, but in with the price comes the novel feeling that, temporarily at least, you and your boat have become one of the prize exhibits.

Ellesmere Port, the 'port' of the Ellesmere Canal, dates from the last decade of the 18th century. The Wirral Line of the Ellesmere Canal met the Mersey here at what had, until then, been simply the small village of Netherpool. The opening of the Birmingham & Liverpool Junction Canal and later the Manchester Ship Canal turned these docks into a transhipment complex of almost unique significance. Happily, surviving neglect typical of the 1960s, much of the infrastructure was saved and incorporated into what was originally known as The Boat Museum, the country's premier collection of preserved inland waterway craft. One can't help but mourn, however, the loss through fire damage in 1970 of Telford's superb 'Winged Warehouses', three blocks of four storey structures which spanned part of the lower basin. Aerial photographs and diagrams exhibited in the museum illustrate the extent of the port in its heyday and emphasise the debt of gratitude owed to the small band of enthusiasts who began the collection of preserved craft which forms the basis of the museum.

Stoak

Soporific rural community despite presence of motorways on its doorstep.

Eating & Drinking

BUNBURY ARMS - village centre, access via bridges 136 or 137. Tel: 01244 301665. *Good Beer Guide* recommended and well-appointed country pub: a much better bet than anything in Ellesmere Port! CH2 4HW

Connections

BUSES - service No. 4 runs Mon-Sat to/from Chester & Ellesmere Port. Tel: 0871 200 2233.

Ellesmere Port

Emphasis on the sea and seafaring ebbs away, but with panoramic views across the Mersey to Liverpool and its cathedrals, it is possible to mitigate against the ugliness of Ellesmere Port's hinterland. The walk in, past tattoo parlours, pawn shops and Polish delis is a dispiriting glimpse of contemporary realities in a sprawling town best known now for its Vauxhall car manufacturing plant.

Eating & Drinking

THE THOMAS TELFORD - Whitby Road (town centre). Tel: 0151 350 3740. Wetherspoons. CH65 8AB

WATERSIDE CAFE - National Waterways Museum. Tel: 0151 355 5017. Open 11am-4pm daily throughout the year. CH65 4FW *Cafe at National Waterways Museum.*

Shopping

Ten minutes walk through a seedy underpass takes you to the town centre. Here, the PORT ARCADES precinct appears half empty, most blue chip retailers having decamped to CHESHIRE OAKS, a salutary bus ride away. Meanwhile, everyday requisites at the vast ASDA, solace in the characterful indoor retail market.

Things to Do

THE NATIONAL WATERWAYS MUSEUM - Tel: 0151 355 5017. Open daily 10-5 Apr-Oct, 11-4 Sat & Sun Nov-Mar. Admission charge. Along with Gloucester and Stoke Bruerne, this is one of three National Waterways Museum sites. Extensive collection of narrow and widebeam inland waterway craft. Cafe and souvenir shop open daily throughout the year. CH65 4FW BLUE PLANET AQUARIUM - Cheshire Oaks. Deepwater antidote to the inherent shallowness of all canals. Tel: 0151 357 8800. Bus connections from EP - see below. CH65 9LF

Connections

BUSES - First service 1 links Ellesmere Port with Liverpool and Chester every 20 minutes Mon-Sat and hourly Sun calling usefully en route at Chester Zoo, Cheshire Oaks retail park, and the Blue Planet Aquarium. Tel: 0871 200 2233. TRAINS - frequent services to Liverpool via Birkenhead and Chester (change at Hooton). Tel: 08457 484950.
TAXIS - Circle Cabs. Tel: 0151 355 2217.

The Llangollen Canal

Boating over the Border

Robin Smithett

THROUGHOUT the summer, narrowboats glide through the broad emerald pastures of the Cheshire Plain, as measuredly as the high cumulus clouds in the wide Cheshire skies above. At Hurleston, a good proportion of them leave the main line of the old Shropshire Union, climb the four locks beside the reservoir embankment, and set off on the voyage to Wales. In terms of popularity 'The Llangollen' is the Blackpool of the canal system, but it has none of that seaside resort's vulgarity, owing its heavy holiday traffic to the enduring charm of its scenery and the vivid drama of its destination.

Hurleston locks raise the canal 34 feet. The reservoir stores water that has flowed down the canal from the River Dee at Horseshoe Falls above Llangollen itself, before it is treated and piped to the kitchen sinks of Crewe. Thank your lucky stars for this water; without it the LMS railway would have closed the canal during the Second World War, because trade had long since ceased. In fact, technically the canal was 'abandoned' and it was only its use as a water channel that saved it from the dereliction suffered by other LMS owned canals under the infamous Act of 1944.

Slowly, a new traffic of pleasure boats began using the canal, and under the 1968 Transport Act the Llangollen Canal (as the section of the old Ellesmere Canal between Hurleston and Llangollen had become known) was classified a 'cruiseway', its position as one of the premier canal holiday routes assured for posterity.

Between Hurleston and Wrenbury the waterway runs, surprisingly, on a North-South axis; subconsciously one expects to be travelling East-West. From bridges 3 and 4 footpaths lead enticingly across the fields to Park Farm where the Sadler's make Snugburys Jersey Ice Cream - Tel: 01270 624830 www.snugburys.co.uk

The locks at Swanley and Baddiley (Map 19) can become congested at busy times; especially with the busy new marina at Swanley Bridge. Patience, patience!

The flow of water down the Llangollen Canal increases the running of the by-washes, causing a gush of water to run across the canal at the foot of locks. To compensate, steer slightly into the overflow. Going downhill, avoid being drawn over to the cill of the by-weir.

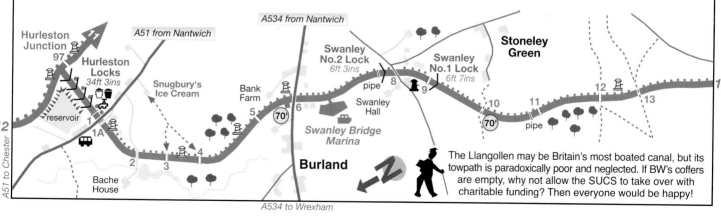

The Llangollen may be Britain's most boated canal, but its towpath is paradoxically poor and neglected. If BW's coffers are empty, why not allow the SUCS to take over with charitable funding? Then everyone would be happy!

WRENBURY is one of the most picturesque ports of call at the English end of the Llangollen Canal. Bridge 20, rebuilt in timber and electrified (operated with a BW key), is equipped with less than discreet traffic lights but it would take more than these to spoil the

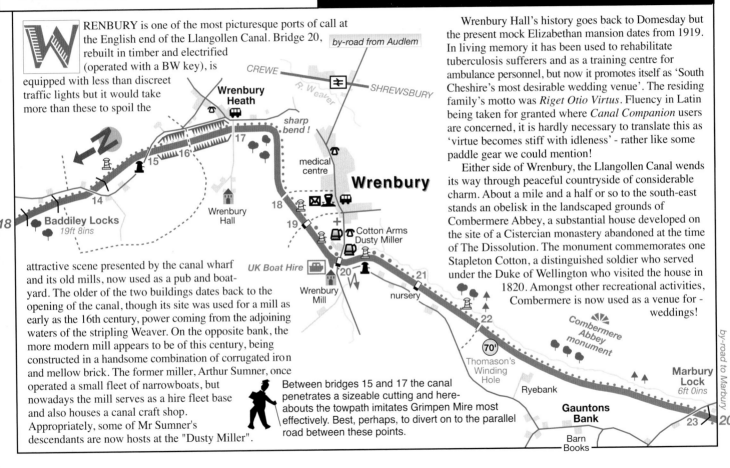

attractive scene presented by the canal wharf and its old mills, now used as a pub and boat-yard. The older of the two buildings dates back to the opening of the canal, though its site was used for a mill as early as the 16th century, power coming from the adjoining waters of the stripling Weaver. On the opposite bank, the more modern mill appears to be of this century, being constructed in a handsome combination of corrugated iron and mellow brick. The former miller, Arthur Sumner, once operated a small fleet of narrowboats, but nowadays the mill serves as a hire fleet base and also houses a canal craft shop. Appropriately, some of Mr Sumner's descendants are now hosts at the "Dusty Miller".

Between bridges 15 and 17 the canal penetrates a sizeable cutting and here-abouts the towpath imitates Grimpen Mire most effectively. Best, perhaps, to divert on to the parallel road between these points.

Wrenbury Hall's history goes back to Domesday but the present mock Elizabethan mansion dates from 1919. In living memory it has been used to rehabilitate tuberculosis sufferers and as a training centre for ambulance personnel, but now it promotes itself as 'South Cheshire's most desirable wedding venue'. The residing family's motto was *Riget Otio Virtus*. Fluency in Latin being taken for granted where *Canal Companion* users are concerned, it is hardly necessary to translate this as 'virtue becomes stiff with idleness' - rather like some paddle gear we could mention!

Either side of Wrenbury, the Llangollen Canal wends its way through peaceful countryside of considerable charm. About a mile and a half or so to the south-east stands an obelisk in the landscaped grounds of Combermere Abbey, a substantial house developed on the site of a Cistercian monastery abandoned at the time of The Dissolution. The monument commemorates one Stapleton Cotton, a distinguished soldier who served under the Duke of Wellington who visited the house in 1820. Amongst other recreational activities, Combermere is now used as a venue for - weddings!

Wrenbury Map 19

A straggling but pleasant village which has its centre around a large green. A strong community spirit manifests itself in the annual, and hugely imaginative scarecrow trail. Otherwise, the canal is arguably its most interesting feature and it is the wharf, with its mellow old mills, which attracts most visitors. Having tapped into a local peat spring in 2004, the Woodlands Brewing Company went into business on a small trading estate adjoining the former goods yard at Wrenbury Station and is now one of the most successful micro-breweries in Cheshire and the border district, though now moved to Nantwich.

Eating & Drinking

DUSTY MILLER - canalside Bridge 20. Tel: 01270 780537. A welcoming and comfortably furnished pub which occupies a converted mill. Wide choice of food and Robinsons ales from Stockport. Nice photographs of old Sumner lorries! CW5 8HG
COTTON ARMS - adjacent Bridge 20. Tel: 01270 780377. Another favourite with boat crews: food, large garden with children's play area. CW5 8HG

Shopping

Well-stocked post office stores down by the village green, five minutes walk from the canal. Open from 7.30am to 8pm Mon-Sat and 8.30am to 1pm Sun. Hot take-away food counter and local Woodlands bottled beer on sale. Tel: 01270 780228.

Connections

TRAINS - Arriva Trains Wales services to/from Crewe and Shrewsbury via Whitchurch and Nantwich. Tel: 08457 484950.
BUSES - service 72 to/from Nantwich and Whitchurch. Tel: 0871 200 2233.

Marbury Map 20

One of those 'quietest places under the sun' that

Wrenbury

we all dream of retiring to. The church lych-gate celebrates "Ye who live mid English pastures green". The tiny green has one of those seats which encircles its tree trunk, just begging to be sat upon. Below the village are two meres. A footpath leads down to the larger and you can watch the antics of the resident wildfowl from its reedy banks. Alternatively, there's a secluded seat in the churchyard overlooking the Big Mere.

Eating & Drinking

THE SWAN INN - village centre. Tel: 01948 662220. Five minutes walk from Bridges 23 or 24. Comfortable country inn with sophisticated menu of bar and restaurant lunches and dinners together with real ales mostly sourced locally. SY13 4LS

Things to Do

BARN BOOKS - Pear Tree Farm. Tel: 01948 663742. Dealer in antiquarian, second-hand and new books. Open Fri-Sun 10am-5pm and also by prior appointment. *www.barnbooks.co.uk* SY13 4HZ

GRINDLEY BROOK is the focal point of this part of the Llangollen Canal. Here are six locks in close proximity, three of them forming a substantial 'staircase' overlooked by a splendid round-bayed lock-keeper's house typical of Telford's architectural style. In fact, the interest at Grindley Brook starts below the bottom lock where a fine skew bridge of blue engineering bricks still carries the trackbed of the old Chester to Whitchurch railway over the canal. A trio of single chambers precedes the staircase, the bottom of which is spanned by the Chester road, and bordered by old mill buildings.

   The activity at Grindley Brook on a Bank Holiday weekend or busy summer's day, when between 60-100 boats may pass through the locks, provides wonderful entertainment for the spectator, if not the cheerful lock-keeper. The staircase locks, in particular, cause considerable congestion (especially on Thursdays and Sundays) with delays of up to three hours often the result, and people react to the hold ups in different ways: some with frustration, some with patient resignation. The secret, of course, is to remember that you're on holiday and supposed to be enjoying yourself! The westbound boater, having climbed some forty feet through the six locks, does at least have twenty lock free miles to look forward to.

   North of Grindley Brook the canal forms the county boundary between Cheshire and Shropshire for a short distance. The 'Sandstone Trail' swells the ranks of towpath walkers on this section. Reeds form a soothing curtain between the path and the water. South of Grindley Brook the canal makes as if to call at the old Shropshire market town of Whitchurch, but then seems to think better of it. A short branch terminated in the centre of town but was abandoned in 1944 and was subsequently, to the town's

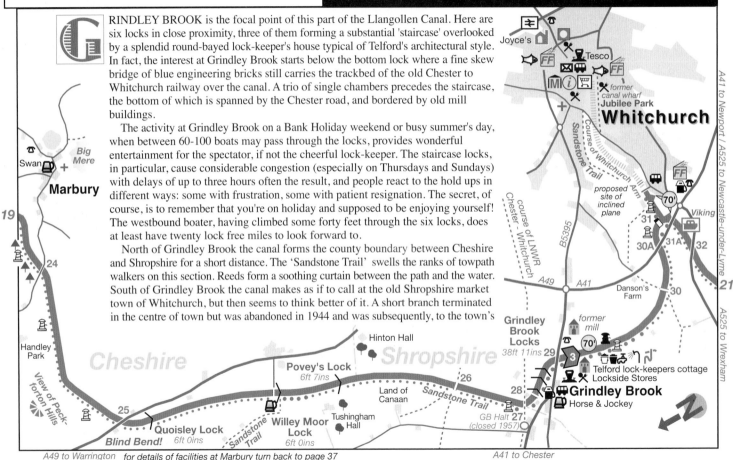

for details of facilities at Marbury turn back to page 37

A49 to Warrington

A41 to Chester

regret, filled in. In 1993, however, a start was made in reclaiming the arm by restoring the first few hundred yards of it to provide moorings for visitors to the town. The next stage involves the construction of two lakes which will ultimately be linked by an inclined plane. Pending this, you can follow the well-surfaced 'Sandstone Trail' into the town, and discover the former wharf, still apparent at the far end of Jubilee Park. In the good old days a weekly cargo of cheese left Whitchurch wharf bound for Manchester in a boat sheeted up with white canvas to deflect the sun's rays.

Whitchurch

Cheese and clocks are Whitchurch's gifts to civilisation. Blue Cheshire cheese is characterised by a marbled effect and is one of the great, tangy blue cheeses in the world. Joyce's, whose handsome premises stand on Station Road, have been manufacturing clocks for eight generations. The tower clock of the prominent St Alkmund's Parish Church is their work and dates from 1849. Whitchurch clocks have been exported all over the world and are to be found on many railway stations and other public buildings. For a town, though, that continues to derive much of its prosperity from clock making, Whitchurch seems a timeless sort of place, immune to the ebb and flow of fashion.

Eating & Drinking
ETZIO - 60 High Street. Tel: 01948 662248. Pizza, pasta and grills adjacent St Alkmund's church. Stylish interior and al fresco decking to rear. Open from 5.30pm Mon-Sat. SY13 1BB
CURSHAWS - Park Avenue. Tel: 01948 663955. Contemporary bar/restaurant (and accommodation) housed in former wharfside building at the edge of Jubilee Park. SY13 1SH
HANNAH - Green End. Tel: 01948 666699. Indian restaurant (& t/a) located on first floor of former Oddfellows Hall erected 1901. SY13 1AD
CHESTERS - Green End. Tel: 01948 662057. Eat in or take-away fish & chips. SY13 1AA
WALKERS - High Street. Tel: 01948 664687. Good value, old-fashioned comfort food in beamy first-floor premises above a bakery. Infinitely maternal waitresses. SY13 1AX
OLD TOWN HALL VAULTS - St Mary's Street. Tel:

01948 662251. Cosy pub which was the birthplace of Sir Edward German, composer of *Merrie England* and other light operatic works. SY13 1QU

Shopping
All services in the town centre, one mile east of the canal. Friday is market day, Wednesday early closing. Farmers Market on the first Saturday in the month. TESCO supermarket by the bus station, plus several good butchers and bakers such as HALE FAMILY BUTCHERS on Green End and WILLIAMS OF WEM at the foot of High Street; launderette on Station Road. W H SMITH on Green End and small bookshop called BOOKSHROP on Bredwood Arcade (by bus station). WHEELBASE bicycle shop on Watergate Street - Tel: 01948 663323.

Things to Do
HERITAGE & TOURIST INFORMATION CENTRE - 12 St Mary's Street. Tel: 01948 665432/664577. Nice exhibitions of local history and personalities such as Edward German and the Victorian illustrator Randolph Caldecott. SY13 1QY

Connections
BUSES - Tel: 0871 200 2233. Service 41 links Whitchurch with Chester bi-hourly and calls at Grindley Brook en route. Service 205 offers a half-hourly Mon-Sat link between the canal arm at Chemistry and the town centre bus park beside Tesco. One service in each direction links Whitchurch with Ellesmere on Wednesdays and Fridays which may be of use for towpath walkers. TRAINS - Arriva Trains Wales services to Crewe (via Wrenbury and Nantwich) and Shrewsbury. Tel: 08457 484950.

TAXIS - Calders Cars. Tel: 01948 666300.

Grindley Brook

Canalside community on the old road from London to Birkenhead.

Eating & Drinking
LOCKSIDE@29 - canalside by staircase locks. Tel: 01948 663385. Internet cafe offering breakfasts, filled baguettes, jacket potatoes etc. See also Lockside Stores below. SY13 4QH
WILLEY MOOR LOCK TAVERN - beside the lock. Tel: 01948 663274. Picturesque - and justifiably popular - *Good Beer Guide* recommended free house reached by motorists via a track off the A49. Good home cooked food and an interesting and ever changing range of ales. Pleasant garden with children's play area. SY13 4HF
HORSE & JOCKEY - just down the B5395 from the locks. Tel: 01948 662723. SY13 4QJ

Shopping
LOCKSIDE STORES (beside the staircase - Tel: 01948 663385)) offer a good range of groceries. Local cheeses and meats are complimented by chutneys and jams, as well as crafts, gifts and Tourist Information. SY13 4QH
Grindley Brook also boasts a petrol station with shop backing onto the bottom lock by Bridge 28. Also here you'll come upon a canalside house selling books and crafts.

Connections
BUSES - service 41 runs approximately bi-hourly throughout the week to Whitchurch in one direction and to Chester in the other. Tel: 0871 200 2233.

SEEMINGLY all alone in the world, the canal crosses remote farmland parallel to the border between Shropshire and the English Maelor, or Flintshire Detached. This curious little pocket of Welshness dates back to Edward I's carving up of the Welsh principalities and Henry VIII's subsequent supression of the Marcher Lords. Such tinkering continues, for, latterly part of Clwyd, this part of Flintshire is now administered by the County Borough of Wrexham.

There are no shops or pubs for miles. With no locks to operate, the boater may be thankful that the occasional lift bridge occupies his attention. All these structures are now built of steel. The wear and tear of passing boats and heavy road traffic have taken its toll on the original wooden structures. The new bridges are also safer to operate, having hydraulically assisted mechanisms instead of the simple, and sometimes unreliable, balance weights of the original bridges. Bridge 39 carries the decaying trackbed of the once proud Cambrian Railways' Oswestry, Ellesmere and Whitchurch line. Opened in 1863, the route just saw out its

centenary before succumbing to the Beeching Axe. The route remained steam-hauled until the end, Manors and Dukedogs predominating.

The Llangollen Canal crosses a region of peat mosses - the Fenn's, Whixall and Bettisfield Mosses National Nature Reserve (see Map 22), which represents the third largest lowland raised bog in Britain. For many years commercial peat cutting was carried out here until English Nature acquired the site in the mid 1990s. Now it is once again home to bog rosemary, large heath butterflies, white-faced darter dragonflies and other rare species. There is access to the Reserve from the towpath near Bridge 44. Other uses were found for the mosses during two world wars: during the first it was a rifle range; during the second a decoy site which could be set ablaze to fool enemy aircraft crews that they were really over Merseyside. When the canal was built across the mosses early in the 19th century, drainage of the peat caused subsidence and the canal company employed a permanent 'Moss Gang' responsible for raising oak-piled clay embankments. Regrettably, the gang became redundant when steel-piling was introduced in the 1960s.

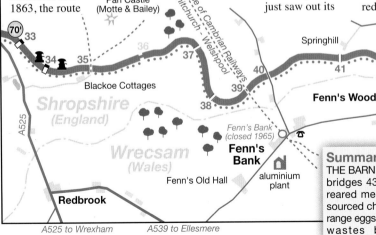

Pan Castle (Motte & Bailey)

Course of Cambrian Railways, Whitchurch - Welshpool

Springhill

Welsh End

Platt Lane

by-road to Whixall

Blackoe Cottages

Shropshire (England)

Fenn's Wood

The Barn

A525

Wrecsam (Wales)

Fenn's Bank (closed 1965)

Fenn's Bank

Fenn's Old Hall

aluminium plant

Redbrook

A525 to Wrexham   A539 to Ellesmere

Summary of Facilities

THE BARN (open Easter to September, 9am-6pm, between bridges 43 and 44) deals in freshly made pies, locally reared meats, Maynards bacon and sausages, locally sourced cheeses, Top House ice cream, vegetables, free range eggs et al. In short, a homely retail oasis in the desert wastes between Whitchurch and Ellesmere!

Whitchurch

Ellesmere

Prees Junction

PREES BRANCH

41

THERE is always something of a 'come hither' element about waterway junctions. However committed you are to the main line a branch seldom fails to tempt you, seeming to dare you to explore whatever languorous charms lie just out of sight. At Whixall the old Prees Branch is no exception, and the remaining mile of what was once a four mile route makes a satisfying diversion from the main canal, often used by discerning boaters for quiet overnight moorings.

Historically, the branch was intended to reach Prees but fell short of its objective by a couple of miles. The actual terminus was established at Quinta Brook. Here a bank of lime burning kilns was erected, for burnt lime was an important farming commodity in the innocent days before chemical fertilizers appeared on the scene. The first, navigable, mile of the Prees Branch serves a marina built on the site of a puddle clay pit from which maintenance men extracted clay to line the canal bed. Beyond the marina its course is now a nature reserve which may be enjoyed - frogbits, yellow water lilies, starworts and all - from the towpath. Two handsome timber lift bridges survive on the arm. An unusual three-storey canal house watches over Prees Junction, its ground floor lying below the level of the canal.

Though there are no facilities as such, Bettisfield repays closer examination. Uphill to the north stands the quaintly Victorian church, designed by G. E. Street in 1874: the stone was quarried on Grinshill, the stained glass is by Clayton & Bell, the tiles Minton, the bells from Taylor's foundry in Loughborough. The buildings at Bettisfield's Beechinged station have at least derived tender loving care from their domestic occupants, the goods shed being an especially attractive conversion. Taraloka is a Buddhist retreat for women.

Hampton Bank is one of the Llangollen Canal's lesser sung engineering achievements; it carries the canal perhaps thirty feet above a headwater of the River Roden, a tributary of the Tern which joins the Severn below Shrewsbury. Larches mask the bank from the prevailing wind. To the south-east, beyond Wem, stands Grinshill; to the north-west the mountains of Wales. Hampton was another place where lime burning for agriculture took place. L. T. C. Rolt moored at Hampton aboard *Cressy* for a month in the summer of 1947, having been thwarted in an attempt to reach Pontcysyllte because of excessive weed and general decay in the canal beyond Ellesmere.

by-road from Whixall

Course   Nature Reserve

70'

Whixall Marina

3

Dobson's Bridge

2

1

Moss Farm

46

45

P

21

by-road from Whitchurch

Fenn's, Whixall & Bettisfield Mosses Nature Reserve

Mosses Trail

Prees Junction

Shropshire (England)

Wrecsam (Wales)

Taraloka

47

48

Bettisfield (closed 1965)

Bettisfield

Bettisfield Boats

49

by-roads to A495

Grinshill

Welsh Hills

Hampton Bank

70'

50

51

52

Lyneal Wharf

53

23

Balmer Heath

N

Shropshire (England)

Crse of Cambrian Rlys

A495 to Whitchurch

Ellesmere - 3 miles

**Time refers to main line, allow 1 hour for return trip along Prees Branch*

42

THE old Shropshire town of Ellesmere embraces its eponymous canal emphatically, a robust response to the commerce it continues to bring to the community coffers two centuries after its conception. Yes, it's worth recalling that what we know glibly as the Llangollen Canal is a term which would be unfamiliar to the canal's promoters. For historically this was the Ellesmere Canal, an ambitious attempt to link the rivers Mersey, Dee and Severn with a main line from Chester to Shrewsbury. In the event, only the Pontcysyllte-Weston Lullingfields section was ever built with, from Welsh Frankton (Map 24), branches to Llanymynech and Ellesmere itself. As it became apparent that the intended main line of the canal would never reach the Dee or Severn, the Ellesmere Canal Company *faute de mieux* cut a canal eastwards from Ellesmere to meet the Chester Canal near Nantwich. Hurleston was reached in the year of Trafalgar.

Forty years later the Ellesmere Canal amalgamated with the Chester Canal and the new Birmingham & Liverpool Junction Canal to form the Shropshire Union Railways & Canal Company. The route from Hurleston to Llangollen was known as the 'Welsh Section' of the Shropshire Union. The term 'Llangollen Canal' didn't gain general currency until British Waterways published a cruising guide under that title in 1956.

Ellesmere became the headquarters of the canal and the company built imposing offices here. Known as Beech House, these premises still preside over the canal junction, though used residentially now, British Waterways being confined to the charmingly higgledy-piggledy maintenance base next door.

continued on page 44

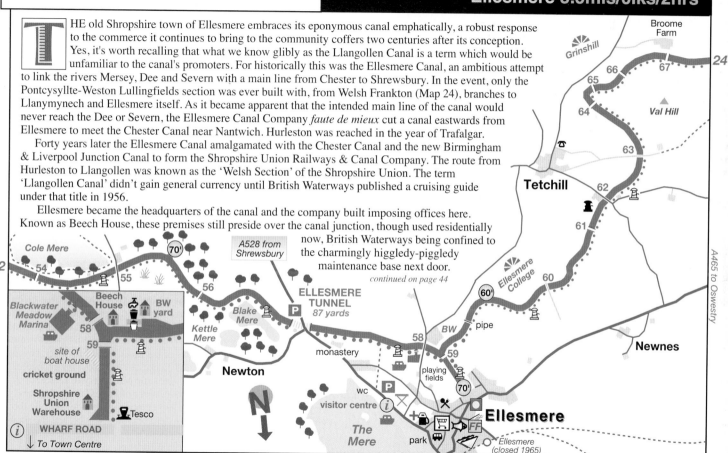

A528 from Shrewsbury

Cole Mere

Beech House

BW yard

Blackwater Meadow Marina

site of boat house

cricket ground

Shropshire Union Warehouse

WHARF ROAD

↓ To Town Centre

Tesco

Kettle Mere

Blake Mere

Newton

ELLESMERE TUNNEL
87 yards

monastery

The Mere

wc

visitor centre

park

Ellesmere College

Tetchill

Newnes

pipe

BW

playing fields

Ellesmere

Ellesmere (closed 1965)

Grinshill

Broome Farm

Val Hill

A465 to Oswestry

for details of facilities at Ellesmere turn to page 45
A528 to Wrexham

Mereside Moorings

Robin Smithett

continued from page 43

Many of the structures which comprise this yard date back to the earliest years of the canal. Particularly notable is the handsome stone drydock with distinctive weathervane in the shape of a narrowboat atop its slate roof. Workshops of timber and stone construction include a joiner's shop, blacksmith's forge and pattern store where wooden templates used for making accurate moulds for iron castings are kept; though, alas, rarely if ever used. Finance has recently been made available to give Ellesmere Yard a facelift with a view - in the air-smoothed syntax of a press release - to: 'realise its potential as a key visitor destination in the town'.

Opposite Beech House a short arm leads to the town wharf. A fresh addition to the canalscape here is the sculpture of an upturned boat, sweetly adorned inside with etched tiles. The arm itself was for many years overlooked by industrial premises that had originally been opened as an ironworks, but which later became a dairy. Now the site is poised for redevelopment - including an 'eco-friendly' branch of Tesco - and one waits nervously to see that the canal's fragile ambience is not overwhelmed.

East of Ellesmere the Llangollen Canal undertakes a hauntingly lovely journey through Shropshire's own 'lakeland'. There are seven lakes, or meres, in the neighbourhood of Ellesmere without inflow or outflow. They were formed at the end of the Ice Age, 10,000 years ago, as the great glaciers retreated and melted waters collected in cups of the land. The meres support a resident population of birds including kingfishers, herons, grebe, Canada geese, coots and moorhens. In winter there's an influx of wildfowl - widgeon, teal, pochard, greylag geese and cormorants. On hot late summer evenings the phenomenon of 'breaking' occurs, as algae rise from the depths to spread a deep blue-green veil upon the surface. Cole Mere and Blake Mere both lie beside the canal, the latter only separated from the waterway by a narrow belt of trees which provide shade for picnics on warm summer days. Forget the helter-skelter rush towards Llangollen, this is one of the true highlights of the canal, a place to linger, unwind and find a real sense of peace. The unique charm of the meres was evoked in Mary Webb's 1926 novel *Precious Bane*. The little Monastery of Our Lady & St Joseph by Ellesmere Tunnel is home to an order of Poor Clare Colletines.

Westwards, the canal rapidly escapes into empty countryside, skirting the playing fields of Ellesmere College, a Woodard boarding school, and the shopless, pub-less village of Tetchill. Side-stepping Val Hill with the dexterity of a 1st XV fly-half, the canal makes for Frankton Junction.

Ellesmere is a rare survival, a small, unspoilt country town with no pretensions. Life seems as slowly lived here as the rythmic lapping of waters on the shores of the meres. Visitors - whether they come by car to feed the ducks, or by boat along the Llangollen Canal - are assimilated without the usual symptomatic rash of tourist traps. Ellesmere's is a long history, traceable back to the Iron Age. The local economy has traditionally been an agricultural one, once there was an ironworks, an important railway junction and a rennet factory, but what the visitor sees today is a late 19th century country town preserved almost in aspic, and all very delightful it is too!

Ellesmere Wharf

Eating & Drinking

BLACK LION HOTEL - Scotland Street. Tel: 01691 622418. Bar and restaurant food in comfortable surroundings opposite the top end of Wharf Road. Real ales. Accommodation. SY12 0EG

PETE'S SANDWICH BAR - Cross Street. Tel: 01691 623414. Down to earth cafe featuring Vermeulen pies and pastries. Archive views of old Ellesmere adorn the walls. SY12 0AR

THAI MERE - High Street. Tel: 01691 624670. Thai restaurant open from 6pm Mon-Sat. SY12 0ES

ASIAN SPICES - Birch Road. Tel: 01691 623689. Indian restaurant and take-away. SY12 0ET
Plenty of additional tea rooms and takeaways as befits a tourist destination.

Shopping

Local retailers were bracing themselves (as we went to press) to see what impact the advent of Tesco would have on their hitherto sleepy town. The council were sanguine - as councils often are - and spoke of a corresponding reduction in carbon footprint. Personally we will still beat a path to VERMEULEN'S delicatessen on Cross Street (Tel: 01691 622521) by the town square. They open around seven in the morning, by which time the aroma of their baking has wafted down to the canal wharf. Their pork pies, still warm to the touch by mid-morning, are simply irresistible, whilst the cold counter contains a mouthwatering array of glazed meats, pates, shellfish and cheeses. Get them to grind some coffee beans for you then dare yourself to leave without a box of their fresh cream cakes.

The indoor market, housed in a handsome Victorian pile opposite the post office, operates on Tuesdays. Thursday is half day. There are several banks in the town and a launderette on Victoria Street. Craft and antique shops feature largely, and you will do well to cast off without some tangible souvenir and a corresponding deficit in your credit card balance.

Things to Do

ELLESMERE INFO-LINK - Wharf Road. Tel: 01691 624488. SY12 0EJ

ELLESMERE VISITOR INFORMATION CENTRE -Mereside. Tel: 01691 622981. SY12 0PA

SHROPSHIRE STEAMBOAT Co. - Tel: 01948 880159. Steam-powered trip boat and rowing boat hire on The Mere.

Connections

BUSES - Tel: 0871 200 2233. Service 53 runs to/from Oswestry at fairly frequent intervals and in doing so provides a link with the nearest railhead at Gobowen. Towpath walkers may also like to note that it crosses the canal at Bridge 13, Map 25. Service 449 also connects Ellesmere to Oswestry but via Whittington, crossing the canal at Bridge 5, Map 24. One service each way on Wednesday and Friday links with Whitchurch.

TAXIS - Jeff's. Tel: 01691 656367.

UT in the middle of the middle of nowhere, Welsh Frankton, or Frankton Junction, was the hub of the Ellesmere canal system. From two junctions in the form of an H, routes radiated to Pontcysllte, Ellesmere, Weston Lullingfields (the intended main line to Shrewsbury) and Llanymynech. The canal continued onwards from there as the Montgomeryshire Canal through Welshpool to Newtown. This route, amounting to some 35 miles, is now known as the Montgomery Canal. In 1936 a breach occurred where the canal crossed the River Perry by aqueduct and the LMS Railway, who owned the canal, chose not to repair it. Eight years later the canal was legally abandoned. In the ensuing fifty years the Montgomery Canal might well have decayed irredeemably had not its scenic splendour been recognised as the canals underwent a revival for pleasure use.

Frankton Locks were restored in 1987 but stood idle for almost ten years, until a further restoration project, involving the construction of a new lock - named after Graham Palmer, founder of the Waterway Recovery Group - allowed boats to reach Perry

Aqueduct. A new brick and steel aqueduct was subsequently built to replace the previous stone structure and the first section of the canal is now navigable for seven miles to Gronwen Wharf; indeed, over half the waterway's thirty-five miles have been restored, as described in the text accompanying Maps 32 to 39.

The canalscape at Frankton is typically self-effacing. Pretty enough with its lock flight, but it's not until you begin to poke about a bit that fragments of the past percolate through. No sign of the warehouse and crane which stood where cars now park by Bridge 69; no toll clerk in the check house by the top chamber; no laughter from the Canal Tavern at the foot of the staircase, though the curious steps and a iron bar are a tangible reminder. A plaque at the tail of the third lock down recalls that L. T. C. Rolt's *Cressy* was converted into a leisure craft at Beech's boat dock in 1929; the dock and workshops lined the offside of the canal below the lock. *Cressy* had been purchased by an uncle of Rolt's from Peates Mill

⚠ Access to the Montgomery Canal via Frankton Locks is restricted to the hours of 12-2pm and must be pre-booked on 01606 723800 no later than 10am the same day; but, better still, further in advance.

The towpath in the vicinity of Maestermyn's boatyard - latterly so eroded that passage was well nigh impossible - *has* been repaired, but without regular loving maintenance it will soon be completely overgrown again!

by-road to Welsh Frankton   A495 to Ellesmere
for details of pubs at Whittington and Hindford turn to page 49

*Allow 1.5 hours for Montgomery Canal to Perry Aqueduct

(see Map 33), having originally been built by the Shropshire Union Canal Carrying Company at Trevor during the First World War. As well as adding extra accommodation, Beech's installed a vertical compound steam engine, for hitherto *Cressy* had been horse-drawn. Rolt accompanied his uncle on the refurbished boat's maiden voyage to Barlaston on the Trent & Mersey south of Stoke-on-Trent one misty morning in March, 1930. With such memories to assimilate, Welsh Frankton makes a good spot to moor overnight. It is not only activity on the canal that has vanished: up the lane the former Free Church chapel of 1890 stands strangled by trees.

Meanwhile, the Llangollen Canal - whose bridge numbers begin again at '1', albeit with the recently appended suffix 'W', just in case you thought you were back at Hurleston! - traverses a low shelf above the valley of the Perry. The Berwyn and Breidden hills of the Border Marches rise up in the west; benignly blue or intimidatingly black according to weather conditions. At Hindford the Cambrian Railways line crosses the canal again, or at least did until 1965. The old bridge abutments are still intact. Even by stopping train it would have taken around half an hour to journey from Fenn's Bank (Map 21) to here. By water it's a six hour voyage; eloquent enough statistics to explain the waning of the canal with the waxing of the railway. Not least for its congenial pub, Hindford is another nice place to moor overnight. At the T junction an old signpost points intriguingly to a place called "Iron Mills".

New Marton locks provide the boater with some not unwelcome exercise. Westbound they are the last to be encountered; eastbound it is some twenty miles to the next one: boating bliss!

Robin Smithett

Frankton locks

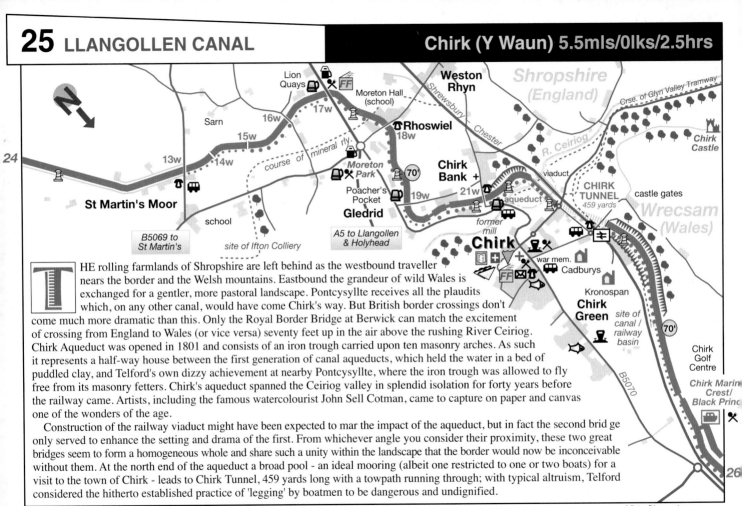

THE rolling farmlands of Shropshire are left behind as the westbound traveller nears the border and the Welsh mountains. Eastbound the grandeur of wild Wales is exchanged for a gentler, more pastoral landscape. Pontcysyllte receives all the plaudits which, on any other canal, would have come Chirk's way. But British border crossings don't come much more dramatic than this. Only the Royal Border Bridge at Berwick can match the excitement of crossing from England to Wales (or vice versa) seventy feet up in the air above the rushing River Ceiriog. Chirk Aqueduct was opened in 1801 and consists of an iron trough carried upon ten masonry arches. As such it represents a half-way house between the first generation of canal aqueducts, which held the water in a bed of puddled clay, and Telford's own dizzy achievement at nearby Pontcysyllte, where the iron trough was allowed to fly free from its masonry fetters. Chirk's aqueduct spanned the Ceiriog valley in splendid isolation for forty years before the railway came. Artists, including the famous watercolourist John Sell Cotman, came to capture on paper and canvas one of the wonders of the age.

Construction of the railway viaduct might have been expected to mar the impact of the aqueduct, but in fact the second bridge only served to enhance the setting and drama of the first. From whichever angle you consider their proximity, these two great bridges seem to form a homogeneous whole and share such a unity within the landscape that the border would now be inconceivable without them. At the north end of the aqueduct a broad pool - an ideal mooring (albeit one restricted to one or two boats) for a visit to the town of Chirk - leads to Chirk Tunnel, 459 yards long with a towpath running through; with typical altruism, Telford considered the hitherto established practice of 'legging' by boatmen to be dangerous and undignified.

Beyond the northern portal of Chirk Tunnel the canal penetrates a wooded cutting of some magnitude. At its far end a winding hole marks the site of a former transhipment wharf between the canal and the narrow gauge Glyn Valley Tramway. Opened in 1873 to serve mines and quarries at the head of the Ceiriog Valley, it also carried passengers. From a separate station alongside the main line, the track curved precipitously down to the valley floor and then ran beside what is now the B4500. The line closed as long ago as 1935, but a group has recently been formed with enthusiastic ambitions of resurrecting this endearing little tramway, initially through interpretation, but eventually by relaying as much of the track as feasible - *www.glynvalleytramway.co.uk*

Whittington — Map 24
NARROWBOAT INN - canalside Bridge 5w, Tel: 01691 661051. Cosy little pub purpose-built by the adjoining boatyard. SY11 4NU

Hindford — Map 24
JACK MYTTON - adjacent Bridge 11w. Tel: 01691 679861. A charming country inn (with spacious gardens beside the canal) which derives its name from an eccentric 19th century squire. Echoes of its namesake's eccentricity percolate down to the present day, but the welcome is effusive, the bar and restaurant food is excellent, and a number of the ales on tap are locally sourced. SY11 4NL

Chirk — Map 25
Many boaters do not bother to visit Chirk, anxious to push on to Pontcysyllte and Llangollen. A pity, because the village centre contains an interesting selection of buildings, including the parish church of St Mary's, the remains of a motte and bailey castle, and a war memorial of Portland stone carved by sculptor and typographer Eric Gill. Look out for the wrought iron sculpture depicting a boat and train on the bridges on the park gate opposite, and the plaque commemorating Billy Meredith, born here in 1874, the 'wing wizard' who won the Welsh Cup with Chirk FC and went on to play for both Manchester clubs and his country on many occasions. Once almost exclusively a mining community, Chirk is now dominated by Cadbury's hot chocolate factory and the adjoining Kronospan timber works which receives incoming raw timber by train from the company's own plantations in Scotland. In the woods between the railway and the canal, where once the diminutive engines of the GVR shunted, stands a small estate of industrial units.

Eating & Drinking
THE HAND HOTEL - Church Street. Tel: 01691 773472. Comfortable and welcoming coaching inn which has long been catering for travellers on Telford's Holyhead road. Buttery, bar and more formal restaurant. Accommodation. LL14 5EY
THE CHIRK TANDOORI - Station Avenue. Tel: 01691 772499. Village centre Indian. LL14 5LU
THE CLUB HOUSE - Tel: 01691 774407. Boaters and golfers rub shoulders at the 19th hole! Access via Chirk Marina. LL14 5AD
BRIDGE INN - Tel: 01691 773213. 'Last pub in England' located beneath the canal embankment just down the hill from Bridge 21w. LL14 5BU
POACHER'S POCKET - canalside Bridge19. Tel: 01691 773250. Popular all-day pub with moorings outside. LL14 5DG
LORD MORETON - Tel: 01691 778888. Bar/restaurant, part of the Moreton Park complex best reached from Bridge 19w. LL14 5DG
LION QUAYS - canalside Bridge 17w. Tel: 01691 684300. Hotel and conference complex thoughtfully providing 'herring-bone' mooring pontoons for boating patrons. SY11 3EW

Holiday Lets
No.3 AQUEDUCT COTTAGES - Tel: 07971 247419. *www.chirkcottage.co.uk* Charming self-catering opportunity in former canal worker's cottage close to the aqueduct. LL14 5DA

Shopping
Make a B-line for McARDLE'S butchers and their wide range of locally sourced produce; they also do delicious take-away hot roast baps, pies etc. The village also supports a baker, pharmacy, Co-op and a branch of the HSBC Bank. MORETON PARK garden centre (adjacent Bridge 19w) offers a wide range of shopping opportunities, including a well-stocked Farm Shop - Tel: 01691 777722.

Things to Do
CHIRK CASTLE - Just over a mile from the north end of the tunnel. Tel: 01691 777701. Over seven hundred years of history and continual habitation to soak up. Admission charge for non National Trust members. Telephone for up to date opening times as these vary from season to season. NT shop, farm shop, restaurant. LL14 5AF

Connections
BUSES - Bryn Melyn service 64 to/from Llangollen (via Froncysyllte) and Glyn Ceiriog. Arriva services to/from Oswestry and Wrexham. Tel: 0871 200 2233.
TRAINS - Arriva Trains Wales services to/from Chester and Holyhead and Shrewsbury, Cardiff and Birmingham. Wrexham & Shropshire trains to/from London Marylebone. Tel: 08457 484950.
TAXIS - Premier. Tel: 01978 861999

The towpath between Whitehouses and Trevor is wide and well surfaced. West of Trevor there are one or two squelchy patches after rain.

A5

27

36w

35w

34w

Crse of GWR: Barmouth-Ruabon

A539

Offa's Dyke Ftp

Trevor Hall

former mill

Plas-yn-Pentre

Garth Trevor

Trevor (closed 1965)

33w

32w

31w

Trevor

N

Froncysyllte

70'

P

Fron Isaf

28w

Pontcysyllte Aqueduct

29w

30w

site of canal / railway basin

WC

FF

former quarry wharf

R. Dee

Cefn Mawr

Cefn Mawr Heritage Trail

Offa's Dyke Footpath

Offa's Dyke

aqueduct

OD Path

Ty Mawr Country Park

A5

26w

27w Cefn Viaduct

Waterloo Tower

Whitehurst Halt (closed 1960)

WHITEHOUSES TUNNEL 191 yards

Pentre

B5605 to Ruabon

25

TREVOR

To Llangollen

32w

Anglo Welsh

31w

To Chirk

aqueduct

BW i

steps down to river bank

dry dock

Dock House

STATION ROAD

The Telford

WC

P

Jones the Boats

70'

NEW ROAD

ENTERING Offa's Dyke country, the Llangollen Canal prepares to make its most dramatic gesture. But first westbound travellers are treated to another tunnel followed by an enchanted passage through a mask of woodland on a shelf above the River Dee. Given the right conditions, the delicious aroma of pinewood fills the air. Between the ivy clad boles of the tall trees there are glimpses of an impressive railway viaduct. Like the canal builders before them, the railway engineers had to contend with the deep valley of the Dee. On the outskirts of Froncysyllte the remains of the former Pen-y-Graig limestone quarries are evident alongside the canal. The actual quarry faces lay uphill to the west and the stone was brought down by a series of tramway inclines on wagons. The tops of six limekilns were at road level with the bottom exits beside the canal. Passing Bridge 28w the canal approaches its climax on a huge embankment built from spoil excavated when Chirk Tunnel was dug.

Pontcysyllte Aqueduct, the most astonishing feat of canal engineering in the world, carries the canal one hundred and twenty feet high across the creaming waters of the River Dee. Superlatives are superfluous, but what is surprising is that the aqueduct is relatively unknown beyond the narrow world of the waterways. Comparatively few people are aware of its existence, let alone able to get their teeth around its knotty consonants. But, pronounced 'Pont-ker-sulth-tee', the bare facts are that it is over 1,000 feet long, 127 feet tall at its deepest point, and consists of an iron trough supported by 18 stone piers. The aqueduct was completed in 1805, the year of Nelson's death at Trafalgar. Along with the Menai Suspension Bridge. It is ranked among Telford's outstanding achievements, though revisionists have lately championed Jessop's contribution.

At Trevor, the canal was to have carried on over the ridge now occupied by the huge chemical plant and then down through Wrexham to the Dee at Chester. Such a course would have required many locks, a very long tunnel or a series of boat lifts. The enormity of this undertaking, coupled with the recession which occurred as an aftermath to the Napoleonic Wars, thwarted the Ellesmere Canal Company's plans to provide a direct canal between the Mersey and the Severn. Telford and his associates would doubtless have overcome the terrain in time, but financially the outlay involved would have broken the bank. In place of the envisaged main line northwards, the canal beyond the aqueduct terminated at a transhipment wharf from where, first a tramway, then later a railway, connected with quarries and collieries on the higher ground towards Ruabon. A further arm described an arc to the east serving chemical, terracotta and iron works in the vicinity. In the Ellesmere Canal's commercial heyday much traffic was generated in the neighbourhood.

Ironically, a canal to Llangollen was not originally planned. Only when it became clear that the main line would never be completed did the company decide to provide a feeder from the River Dee at Llantisilio to the canal at Trevor. The cutting of a canal along the steep slopes of the Vale of Llangollen posed considerable problems and this was the last section of the canal to be completed, over two years after the aqueduct had been opened to traffic. Technicalities apart, it is one of the most memorable lengths of canal in the country, an aquatic mountain odyssey of unparalleled loveliness.

Froncysyllte

A mountain goat of a village famed for its male voice choir. If your legs are up to it, it's worth following the zig-zagging lane up to the crest of the ridge for spectacular views across the Dee Valley and up into the Vale of Llangollen.

A fish & chip shop (open all day and offering cooked breakfasts too), roadside pub, and an Indian take-away (Tel: 01691 774858) are all that 'Fron' currently offers to passers-by, be they on the Holyhead road or the canal to Llangollen.

Connections

BUSES - Bryn Melyn services to/from Llangollen and Chirk, Ruabon and Wrexham. Tel: 0871 200 2233.

Trevor

Chemical works spill down the hillside and the basin is hard by a housing estate, but the canal shrugs off such intrusions and a large car park reflects the popularity of the aqueduct as a visitor attraction. Leaflets are available locally to guide you round the varied delights of Cefn Mawr Heritage Trail and Ty Mawr Country Park. Cefn Druids, one of the oldest football clubs in the Principality, play at the nearby Plas Kynaston Lane ground.

Pontcysyllte Aqueduct

Eating & Drinking

TELFORD INN - Tel: 01978 820469. Canalside adjoining the Anglo Welsh base. Popular with both boaters and land based visitors, the 'Telford' is known for its home made steak pies. Canalside seating area and a children's playground. LL20 7TT

Holiday Lets

DOCK HOUSE - Tel: 0117 304 1122. Self-catering for up to five persons at Trevor canal wharf. Operated by Anglo Welsh. LL20 7TX

Shopping

There is a small general store and off licence some 200 yards from the canal basin, whilst groceries, gifts, cards, guides and maps are available from the Anglo Welsh boatyard shop.

Things to Do

TRIP BOATS - Aqueduct Cruises (Tel: 01978 823215) and Jones the Boats (Tel: 01691 690322) both offer regular vertigo-defying cruises across Pontcysyllte Aqueduct.

Connections

BUSES - Arriva service 5 every quarter of an hour (Mon-Sat) hourly (Sun) to/from Llangollen and Wrexham from stops on the A539. Tel: 0871 200 2233.

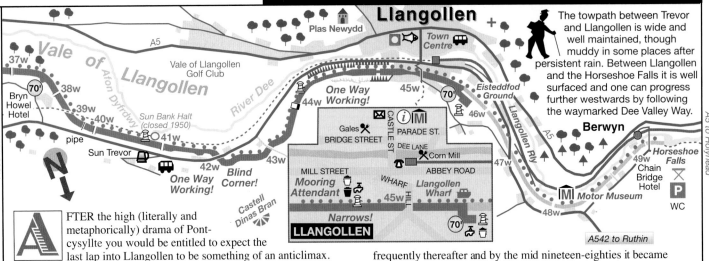

The towpath between Trevor and Llangollen is wide and well maintained, though muddy in some places after persistent rain. Between Llangollen and the Horseshoe Falls it is well surfaced and one can progress further westwards by following the waymarked Dee Valley Way.

A FTER the high (literally and metaphorically) drama of Pont-cysyllte you would be entitled to expect the last lap into Llangollen to be something of an anticlimax. Happily, this is not the case; rather, the canal treats you to all the wild majesty that the celebrated Vale of Llangollen can muster. Great buttresses of limestone cliffs tower above conifer plantations, making Hurleston and gentle green Cheshire seem an eternity away. When the weather is kind, you find yourself constantly lifting your eyes up into the hills, where sunlight gives the heather-clad ridges the clarity of well executed marquetry. But Wales wouldn't be Wales if it weren't for the frequent, dripping Celtic mists that come creeping up the valley of the Dee, muffling boat exhausts and dampening the woods, but not the spirits.

Not surprisingly, the section between Trevor and Llangollen has a history of breaches. In 1945 the bank collapsed by Bridge 41w and the adjoining railway was swept away. Before any warning could be given, a goods train plunged into the gap and the driver was killed. Bursts occurred more frequently thereafter and by the mid nineteen-eighties it became apparent to British Waterways that this section would, effectively, have to be rebuilt. Nowadays the canal bed is concrete-lined, under drained and fitted with a waterproof membrane following an extensive improvement programme.

Never exactly wide, the canal narrows as it approaches Llangollen with 'one way working' along three short sections. Boaters need to be patient in high season, and a good deal of frustration can be saved simply by sending a member of your party ahead to check if a boat is approaching in the opposite direction. On the final approach to Llangollen a Mooring Attendant supervises visiting boats, for berths are always at something of a premium in Llangollen, especially at the height of the season. You can stay for up to four hours free of charge as long as you depart no later than 5pm. Ovenight stays of up to 24 hours currently cost £6; 48 hours £12. This isn't quite as expensive as it may sound because each berth - be it linear alongside the towpath east of Llangollen Wharf, or in the mooring basin west of Bridge 45w - is equipped with water and electricity supplies.

Running above the grey roofs of the town the canal reaches the old Llangollen Wharf where the warehouse serves as a base for the horse-drawn boats which ply the final, narrow, shallow section up to Horseshoe Falls. A winding hole beyond the warehouse marks the turning point for all powered craft.

Finally, accompanied by the River Dee and the gently puffing trains of the restored steam railway, the feeder canal continues for another couple of miles beyond Llangollen to Llantisilio. In many ways it seems entirely appropriate that boaters should have to stretch their legs to reach what amounts to the end - but is really the beginning - of the canal. Horseshoe Falls, though, with its great crescent shaped weir, overlooked by the bulk of Llantisilio Mountain and the higher peaks of the Berwyns, is a point of pilgrimage which should not be eschewed. Here, by the tiny valve house that meters the flow of water into the canal, it is time to savour the forty-four mile journey from Hurleston and all those ingredients which make the Llangollen Canal one of the great inland waterway experiences in the world.

Llangollen
Map 27

Once a year in early July, this little grey-slated Welsh town takes on a cosmopolitan atmosphere, as singers and dancers in colourful national dress take part in the famous Eisteddfod. In truth, the town is busy with tourists all summer long, as it has been since the 18th century, when early travel writers like Hazlitt and Borrow discovered the wild charm of the Vale of Llangollen. Arguably, Llangollen's heyday coincided with the residence here of the 'Ladies of Llangollen' when such august figures as Wordsworth, Sir Walter Scott and the Duke of Wellington were regular visitors. The canal wharf lies over the river from the bulk of the town, but it's just a short walk over the creaming Dee via the graceful Bishop Trevor Bridge to the centre.

Eating & Drinking
THE CORN MILL - Dee Lane. Tel: 01978 869555. Look no further than this stylish modern restaurant & bar housed within an 18th century mill whose water wheel still turns for the entertainment of diners. Balcony seating for warm days with views across the Dee to the nostalgic shufflings and shuntings of Llangollen's steam trains. LL20 8PN
GALES WINE BAR - Bridge Street. Tel: 01978 860089. Characterful wine bar offering food and also accommodation. LL20 8PF

CAESAR'S - Dee Lane. Tel: 01978 860133. Characterful little restaurant by the river bridge. LL20 8PN
CHAIN BRIDGE HOTEL - canalside Bridge 49w. Tel: 01978 860215. Bar and restaurant food for non-residents with views over the Dee at 'un-navigable' end of the canal. LL20 8BS
SUN TREVOR - adjacent Bridge 41w. Tel: 01928 860651. Pleasant roadside pub with good moorings available away from the crush at Llangollen. LL20 8EG

Shopping
Predictably, there's a surfeit of gift shops, yet in amongst all the dross there are many genuinely attractive craft outlets. Plenty of food shops too, notably JAMES BAILEY'S delicatessen (offering hugely tasty Welsh Oggies) and the butcher D.M. PIERSON, both on Castle Street. Market day is Tuesday, there are branches of NatWest, Barclays and HSBC banks, and you'll find a useful launderette on Regent Street (the A5) where there is also a small Somerfield supermarket.

Things to Do
TOURIST INFORMATION CENTRE - The Chapel, Castle Street. Tel: 01978 860828. LL20 8NU
LLANGOLLEN WHARF - The Wharf. Tel: 01978 860702. Base for motor-boat and horse-drawn trip boats. Gift shop and cafe. LL20 8TA
LLANGOLLEN MUSEUM - Parade Street. Tel: 01978 862862. LL20 8PW
LLANGOLLEN RAILWAY - station riverside, next to the canal wharf. Tel: 01978 860979/860951. Daily service (May to October) of steam hauled trains through delightful Dee Valley scenery to Carrog (with an extension planned to Corwen). Combined rail/boat trips. Gift shop and refreshment room at station overlooking the Dee. LL20 8SN
PLAS NEWYDD - Hill Street. Tel: 01978 861314. This delightful black and white timbered house set in charming gardens was the home of the 'Ladies of Llangollen', two daughters of aristocratic Irish families who lived here from 1779 to 1831. Admission charge. Open daily Easter to October. LL20 8AW
And all around are hills crying out to be climbed. A particularly fine walk leads from Bridge 45w to the 1000ft summit of Castell Dinas Bran.

Connections
BUSES - Bryn Melyn services to/from Chirk. Arriva services to/from Wrexham, Corwen, Bala and Barmouth. Tel: 0871 200 2233.
TAXIS - Premier. Tel: 01978 861999.

The Middlewich Branch

TO subconsciously relegate the Middlewich Branch to the back of your mind as an unspectacular but necessary link in the waterways of the North-west would be unjust, for this is a rumbustious canal, carrying you loftily above the snaking valley of the River Weaver, and presenting you with expansive views towards a horizon bounded by Delamere Forest and the Peckforton Hills. Church Minshull looks - from the canal's elevated position - like a toy village embracing the river's luxuriant banks. Tom and Angela Rolt enjoyed an extended stay here in the fateful autumn of 1939 while Tom worked for

rear. Several sizeable farms border the canal, their fields filled with black and white milking herds or cut red by the plough in a ruddy shade of corduroy. Near Bridge 22, woods partially obscure the Top Flash, a subsidence induced lake beside the Weaver. The West Coast Main Line, busy with silver-coloured Virgin trains for the most part, crosses the canal. To the south-east lies a forgotten, older transport route, a Roman road which linked the early salt mines at Nantwich and Middlewich.

Rolls-Royce at Crewe.

Keep your eyes peeled for the Jacobean style house alongside Bridge 14. Between bridges 18 and 19 former canal horse stables have been fetchingly refurbished as living quarters after years lying derelict. Note how the adjoining canal cottage boasts three storeys to the

Completely rural and with an adequate towpath, the Middlewich Branch is good walking territory. A number of footpaths and quiet lanes link with the towpath but it is frustratingly difficult to walk beside the River Weaver. The closest approach can be made through woodlands by Bridge 19.

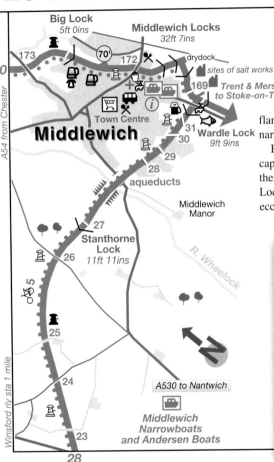

MIDDLEWICH was always a centre of boating activity in commercial carrying days and remains busy today, being situated on both the Cheshire and Four Counties Rings, two of the most popular cruising circuits. A pair of busy hire bases adds to the through traffic. The three central locks are all deep - a total rise (or fall) of over 30 feet - and are bordered by compounds of stacked pallets and the uninspiring architecture of modern industrial units; a far cry from the salty scenes of the past when Seddons and Cerebos were at their zenith and a forest of flaring chimney stacks supported the Middlewich sky. Seddons operated a fleet of some twelve narrowboats until 1960, some having remained horse-drawn until well after the war.

Big Lock lives up to its name, recalling the original determination that the canal should be capable of taking widebeam craft from the ports of the Mersey as far inland as Middlewich. But then the tunnels north of Anderton were built too narrow and the die was effectively cast. Big Lock's gates used to be operated by a curious drum and chain mechanism and one misses such eccentricity in these days of increasingly standardised lock gear.

Middlewich

Middlewich attempts visibly to raise its game, and the annual Folk & Boat Festival proves increasingly popular, yet the ruined and seemingly unlettable and unrefurbishable canal wharf continues to set the unfortunate tone for this salt-making town. The most most interesting building remains the parish church of St Michael whose tower is scarred with missiles unleashed during the Civil War.

Eating & Drinking

KINDERTON'S - adjacent Bridge 172. Tel: 01606 834325. Sophisticated (for Middlewich!) contemporary restaurant. CW10 0JE
THE NARROWBOAT - Lewin Street. Tel: 01606 738087. Welcoming town centre pub with a well-appointed dining room. CW10 9AS

ALHAMBRA - Wheelock Street. Tel: 01606 841549. Chinese. CW10 9AG.
KINGS LOCK FISH & CHIPS - Tel: 01606 832020.

Shopping

There's a Tesco Express (with a cash machine), Somerfield supermarket (fairly well hidden at the back of Wheelock Street) and a branch of Lidl (at its far end). NatWest and Barclays banks. A small market is held every Tuesday, whilst a number of shops close at midday on Wednesdays.

Connections

BUSES - Arriva service 42 links Middlewich with Congleton and Crewe (for the railway station) hourly Mon-Sat. Tel: 0871 200 2233.
TAXIS - Sid's. Tel: 01606 833815.

WOODLAND interludes and subsidence-induced flashes characterise the Trent & Mersey's serene passage through the Dane Valley. Hereabouts the river (having risen in the Derbyshire Peak District on the flank of Axe Edge) has grown sluggish with age, meandering about its level valley in a series of lazy loops; one moment it's hard by the canal, the next away across the pasturelands of milking herds. The soil here is soft and the Dane carves deep banks made shadowy by alder and willow. The canal shares the valley with a Roman Road known as King Street and a now lightly used railway which once sported a 'push & pull' service between Crewe and Northwich, but these other transport modes barely intrude upon what is otherwise a long, relaxing pound. At Higher Shurlach commerce rears its perfidious head in the shape of a giant distribution depot for Morrisons. The moist aromas of bread-making issue from Roberts 'Red Rose' bakery who run their own brass band.

The most curious feature of this section of the canal are the flashes bordering the main channel to the south of Bridge 181. That nearest the bridge was once filled with the submerged wrecks of abandoned narrowboats, an inland waterway equivalent of Scapa Flow. Many of the boats were brought here and sunk *en masse* during the Fifties in circumstances as controversial - in canal terms that is - as the scuttling of the German Fleet after the First World War. In what was probably a book-keeping exercise, British Waterways rid themselves of surplus narrowboats in a number of watery graves throughout the system. In recent years the wrecks have been raised and taken off for restoration. One generation's cast-offs become the next's prized possessions.

Whatcroft Hall is topped by a handsome dome. By Bridge 179 its old lodge houses are prettily half-timbered. In the woods between bridges 176 and 177 the mangled remains of old wagon tipplers hint at the existence of clay or puddle pits. Note also how the bridges along this length are flat topped so that they could be relatively easily raised in the event of subsidence.

Croxton Aqueduct was rebuilt to broad-beam dimensions in 1891 so as to permit wide beam craft to work between Anderton and Middlewich. However, after being damaged by flooding in the Thirties, it reverted to its present narrow status.

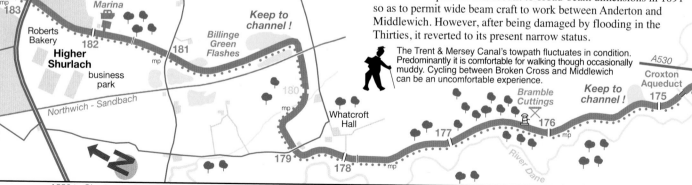

The Trent & Mersey Canal's towpath fluctuates in condition. Predominantly it is comfortable for walking though occasionally muddy. Cycling between Broken Cross and Middlewich can be an uncomfortable experience.

WINCHAM and Anderton introduce industrial overtones to this section of the Trent & Mersey Canal, but some canal travellers may welcome the intrusion of factories into the peaceful landscape.

This part of Cheshire was the centre of Britain's salt industry and the canal negotiates a scarred landscape destabilised over the years by salt extraction. In 1958 a new length of canal had to be dug at Marston to by-pass a section bedevilled by subsidence. Lion Salt Works was the last place in Britain to produce salt by the traditional method of evaporating brine in open pans. It closed in 1986 but is now gradually being restored as a working museum and visitor centre.

Of all the celebrated 'Seven Wonders of the Waterways', Anderton Lift is arguably the most ingenious. It performs the role of raising or lowering craft through the fifty foot disparity in level between the Trent & Mersey Canal and the Weaver Navigation. The Lift dates from 1875 and was designed by Edwin Clark. Its imposing framework contains two water-filled caissons, each capable of holding a pair of narrowboats.

Anderton
Eating & Drinking
STANLEY ARMS - opposite Anderton Lift . Tel: 01606 75059. CW9 6AG
LIFT CAFETERIA - canalside. Tel: 01606 786777. CW9 6FW
THE MOORINGS - Anderton Marina. Tel: 01606 79789. CW9 6AJ
Things to Do
ANDERTON BOAT LIFT - Tel: 01606 786777. Canalside visitor centre celebrating The Lift and local canals. A widebeam trip boat offers 30 minute trips up or down The Lift. CW9 6FW *Frequent buses run to/from Northwich.*

Marston
Eating & Drinking
SALT BARGE - Bridge 193. Tel: 01606 43064. CW9 6ES
Things to Do
LION SALT WORKS - Tel: 01606 41823. Open afternoon daily. CW9 6ES

Broken Cross
Eating & Drinking
OLD BROKEN CROSS - Bridge 184. Tel: 01606 40431. CW9 7EB
Shopping
Co-op 10 minutes west of Bridge 184.

Fuller coverage of the canals in this area is contained in the Cheshire Ring Canal Companion

30

The Montgomery Canal

HOWEVER popular the Montgomery Canal may become, as restoration forges ahead, its topographical hinterland will remain remote, creating a welcome sense of isolation. After a burst of activity generated by Frankton Locks, the junction with the intended main line to Shrewsbury, Graham Palmer Lock and the new aqueduct over the River Perry (see Map 24), the canal soon loses itself in a timeless agricultural landscape, the Berwyn and Breidden hills defining the western horizon. Accommodation bridges are conspicuous by their absence. Perhaps the canal followed the boundary between farms.

At Heath Houses the Shrewsbury-Chester railway crosses the canal and a derelict arm extends into the reedy precincts of a former transhipment basin, used in latter years as a bone works. In the mid 19th century a short-lived packet boat service operated between Newtown and Heath Houses to connect with the railway. The high-chimnied station house of Rednal & West Felton remains intact and used as a private

dwelling complete with a valance-canopied timber goods shed in the grounds! Back on the canal, the equally quaint brick and timber building abutting Bridge 74 was a passenger terminal for users of the passenger boat. Apparently the Wolverhampton Swift Packet Boat Company advertised a schedule of just over five hours for their boat to cover the 32 miles and 22 locks involved!

Running parallel to a busy by-road (though one which it might be preferable to walk along - see below) and skirting the edge of a wood of silver birch, the canal makes its quiet way to Queen's Head, a small roadside community on Telford's road to Holyhead, the A5. In the canal's working days there were mills here and a sand wharf linked to a narrow gauge railway.

From 1996 to 2003 Queen's Head marked a temporary terminus in restoration terms. Aston Locks had been restored for use by boats, but controversy surrounded the passage of the canal through an area designated as being of Special Scientific Interest on account of the rare plants and insects which thrive here. The resultant truce involves responsibilities on the part of passing boaters. Below Aston Locks the towpath has been resurfaced, but how long before the rampant banks of butterbur and balsam encroach?

The towpath is in reasonably good condition between Frankton Junction and Maesbury Marsh: comfortable for walkers, acceptable for cyclists. Between bridges 74 and 76, however, the parallel road is more comfortable underfoot, though be wary of the traffic.

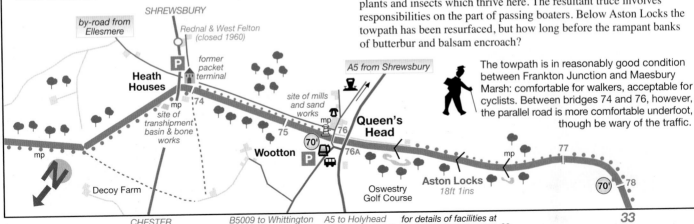

for details of facilities at Queen's Head turn to page 63

Maesbury Marsh

REVELLING in its rural isolation, the Montgomery Canal comes upon Maesbury Marsh, a quintessential country wharf with an inn, stables, boatmen's cottages and dock; the waterway equivalent of a country station before the Beeching era. Business used to be brisk at Maesbury Marsh, for this was the nearest wharf to Oswestry, and many commodities came and went through here before the railway reached the town. Sycamore House, the agent's residence, bears a family likeness to Beech House back at Ellesmere.

Beyond lift-bridge No.81 is the short arm which once led to Peates Mill. Sadly, the mill ceased operating in 2002 - though Lloyd's more modern animal feeds plant continues to be very much in business near Bridge 83; the company also operate mills at Wrexham, Darlington and Langport (Somerset). For their part, Peates once operated a fleet of narrowboats - not least *Cressy* of *Narrow Boat* fame- having purchased eleven craft from the Shropshire Union Company when they ceased trading in 1921. Soon, though, the development of the motor lorry made it unviable to continue carrying by canal. The grain Peates imported by way of Ellesmere Port took three or four days to reach the mill by horsedrawn boat, whereas the company's 13 ton lorry, purchased in 1932, was able to make two round trips to the port in a day.

It is hardly surprising, then, that trade had all but evaporated from the Montgomery Canal well before the fateful breach of 1936. But in the next two or three miles of canal you come upon the remains of some of the key industries which made it successful for a time at least. The wharf at Bridge 82 was linked by tramway to a number of collieries up on Sweeney Mountain, whilst at Crickheath Wharf another tramway connected with quarries at Llynclys and Whitehaven.

By the beginning of 2009, the canal's navigable status was in the process of being restored as far as Crickheath Wharf, beyond which there is the lowered road bridge No.86 to contend with before Pant can be reached. Lift-bridge 82A is an entirely new structure, handsomely erected in the timber style favoured along the Llangollen Canal. For many years the canal south-west of Crickheath has been largely dry, its bed burgeoning with nettles, saplings and reeds.

The canal isn't the only transport mode being slowly brought back to life. Don't be surprised if you hear a steam whistle in the neighbourhood of Bridge 87, for a section of the old Cambrian Railways line has been re-opened from Llynclys.

Pant was the scene of more interaction between water and rail. The standard gauge Cambrian Railways squeezed through the gap between the canal and the hillside and a station perched over the waterway by Bridge 88. Narrow gauge mineral lines came swooping down from the hillside quarries - hence the extra arch on the offside of the bridge. By Bridge 91 there is a bank of well preserved limekilns.

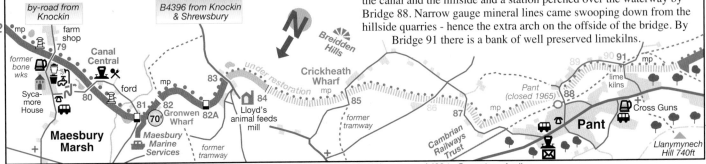

Maesbury Marsh

Robin Smithett

Queen's Head — Map 32

Eating & Drinking
QUEEN'S HEAD - canalside Bridge 76. Tel: 01691 610255. Well-appointed 'all-day' pub serving a wide choice of food and real ales. SY11 4EB

Shopping
In such remote climes you may be grateful for WEST FELTON STORES (Tel: 01691 610863 - SY11 4EA) a mile south along the pavemented old A5; or take advantage of the bus below!

Connections
BUSES - Arriva service 70 operates half-hourly Mon-Sat and bi-hourly Sun to/from Oswestry and Shrewsbury. Tel: 0871 200 2233.

Maesbury Marsh — Map 33
Meresberie in the Domesday Book straddles the River Morda, a tributary of the Vyrnwy and there is evidence of Wat's Dyke a precursor of Offa's. St John's church is one of those sweet little pre-fabricated corrugated iron 'Tin Tabernacles' which traveller's on the canals seem to encounter more frequently than most.

Eating & Drinking
NAVIGATION INN - alongside Bridge 79. Tel: 01691 672958. Friendly welcome, comfortable and well-appointed, excellent bar and restaurant food, Wood's Shropshire-brewed ales. SY10 8JB *See also Canal Central below.*

Shopping
CANAL CENTRAL - adjacent Bridge 80. Tel: 01691 652168. Goodness - the canal system has witnessed scant evidence of imaginative entrepreneurship such as this since the late nineteen-seventies! Splendid combination of village shop (specialising in locally-sourced items of viands and victuals, Welsh/Shropshire beers, quality wines etc) and coffee shop/tea room (poached eggs, bacon butties, cottage pie, soups, cakes and crumpets) housed in an eco-friendly Scandinavian style building beside the canal. Self-catering accommodation also available. SY10 8JG

Connections
BUSES - Arriva service 576 connects approx bi-hourly, Mon-Sat with Oswestry and Shrewsbury (via Ruyton XI Towns). Tel: 0871 200 2233
TAXIS - Prestige. Tel: 01691 671163.

Pant — Map 33
Thus far, it seems, the local wags have resisted the urge to append a rogue S to the village name-boards; though one suspects it is only a matter of time, and that in this day and age they'll probably use a Z. But Pant does not deserve to be ridiculed, for even though it's in Shropshire, it is a typically Welsh wayside village, more chapel than church, and well-sited to take advantage of a fully restored canal in years to come. Buzzards call over the wooded flanks of Llanymynech Hill and there are steep paths up to its nature reserve.

Eating & Drinking
CROSS GUNS - village centre. Tel: 01691 830821. SY10 9QR

Shopping
Co-op stores with post office at the top of Station Road most easily reached from Bridge 88.

Things to Do
CAMBRIAN RAILWAYS TRUST - Llynclys. Tel: 01691 831569. Ambitious plans are on the table to re-open the railway between Gobowen and Llanymynech. At present just a short stretch is in operation (mostly at weekends during the summer months) from Llynclys north of Pant. SY10 8LL

Connections
BUSES - Arriva services 71 and 445, plus Tanat Valley D71, give Pant a rather better than hourly Mon-Sat link with Oswestry. Tel: 0871 200 2233.

THE canal skirts the foot of the limestone eminence of Llanymynech Hill. Probably worked for its mineral deposits as long ago as the Iron Age, it now has a golf course on its summit, notable in that fifteen of its holes are in Wales and three in England. Ian Woosnam started paying on its thymy fairways at the age of nine, Barbara Pym also golfed up there. At the point where a former railway (known as 'Rock Siding') crossed the canal, it comes becomes navigable again for a short distance and a trip boat plies from Llanymynech Wharf. A high chimney heralds the approach to the hill's eponymous village, and the indents of old wharves eat into the offside bank. The chimney was the flue for a Hoffman kiln used for the continuous burning of limestone. If you have ever travelled on the Settle & Carlisle railway you'll have passed a similar installation north of Settle. There is also one preserved at the Prestongrange Museum in East Lothian.

Bridge 93 is still intact in its hump-backed innocence, but the by-road to Tanat which crossed it has been directed across the bed of the canal. A few hundred yards to the west the canal joins a road to cross the trackbed of the old branchline railway to Llanfyllin. Carreghofa, a typical GWR halt, lay on the other side of the road, deep in a cutting. When the railway was built a temporary aqueduct was constructed pending completion of the permanent one so as not to interrupt canal traffic, and its abandoned arms are still to be seen disappearing into the undergrowth. A similar phenomenon occurs at Bloxwich on the Wyrley & Essington Canal.

Carreghofa Locks mark the

Between bridges 93 and 103 the canal, for the time being at least, remains unnavigable. The towpath has been resurfaced between Llanymynech and Carreghofa. Elsewhere the towpath - shared between Llanymynech and Four Crosses with the Offa's Dyke Path - is in adequate condition for walkers, but not suitable for cyclists. Between Maerdy Bridge and Arddleen vegetation has a tendency to take over at the height of summer. Care needs to be exercised when crossing the A483 at the site of flattened bridges 102 and 103 for the traffic is both heavy and fast.

original junction between the Llanymynech Branch of the Ellesmere Canal and the Eastern Branch of the Montgomeryshire Canal. A wharfinger's office adjoins the upper lock, the lockhouse's modest two-storey road frontage masks a much more imposing rear. It is at Carreghofa that westbound travellers enjoy their first encounter with the Montgomeryshire Canal's unique segmented paddle gear.

An embankment with flood arches, bisected by another flattened road, leads to Vyrnwy Aqueduct, the canal's major engineering structure. Erected to the design of John Dadford in 1796, it owes more to the Brindley school of aqueduct construction than Dadford's contemporary, Telford. One of its arches collapsed soon after its opening and, in 1823, George Buck - later to build the magnificent railway viaduct at Stockport - was brought in to strengthen it. Just when he thought he had finished, the walls of the aqueduct bulged and appeared to be collapsing. Buck is said to have smote the ground in despair, but with the help of additional iron tie bars - still prominent to this day - the aqueduct has more or less stood its ground ever since. Cogitate upon this colourful past as you lean upon the parapet of the present and watch the waters of the Vyrnwy glide below. For a more embracing view of the aqueduct, stroll down to the adjacent road bridge from 'bridge' 96.

A dog-leg bend takes the canal off the aqueduct past a handsomely refurbished salt warehouse built to last from local stone. Bridge 98, which carried the carriage road to Pentreheylin Hall, has some ornate woodwork. Arcing round the attractive hillside of Bryn Mawr, the canal reaches Four Crosses where there were separate wharves and winding holes either side of Bridge 100. Twice in the next three miles the A483 slices across the bed of the canal, presenting a difficult challenge to restoration.

Llanymynech — Map 34

Road traffic holds this former quarrying village hostage, bludgeoning the bucolic sensibilities of canal travellers poking their heads up the steps of Bridge 92. Walk down one side of the main street and you are in England, cross the road and you are in Wales. In common with all these border communities, the locals come over as a blurred mixture of Celt and Anglo Saxon; presumably the result of all that illicit inter-marrying down the ages. Speaking of progeny, the village's most famous native is Richard Roberts, inventor of the gasometer. Railway enthusiasts may recognise Llanymynech as the western terminus of the Shropshire & Montgomeryshire Railway, one of Colonel Stephens' impecunious outfits beloved of L. T. C. Rolt, who once propelled a platelayer's trolley from Kinnerley to Llanymynech and back in the same time scheduled for the trains; a statistic which says more about the generosity of the timetable than about Rolt's athletic prowess.

Eating & Drinking
CROSS KEYS - Tel: 01691 831585. Well-appointed pub which straddles the border. Good choice of food and local beer, and comfortable and inexpensive accommodation too. SY22 6EA
BRADFORD ARMS - Tel: 01691 830582. Homely pub offering food and B&B. SY22 6EJ.
GOLDEN VALLEY - Tel: 01691 830426. Chinese take-away. SY22 6EZ
BENGAL SPICES - Tel: 01691 830170. Indian restaurant and take-away. SY22 6ER

Shopping
Like so many of their brethren, the village stores had just closed last time we came to research. Sandwiches etc are obtainable from a small outlet and newspapers from another, otherwise press on to Four Crosses or go back to Pant.

Things to Do
LLANYMYNECH WHARF VISITOR CENTRE - Tel: 01691 830506. Emergent community-run attraction with trip boat, adjoining industrial heritage area, and nature reserve.

Connections
BUSES - Tanat Valley service D71 links Llanymynech to Welshpool and Oswestry Mon-Sat, whilst Arriva service 445 provides a few additional services between Llanfyllin and Oswestry. Arriva service 71 connects hourly, Mon-Sat with Four Crosses, Pant and Oswestry Tel: 0871 200 2233.

Four Crosses — Map 34

Eating, Drinking & Accommodation
THE FOUR CROSSES - Tel: 01691 831643 - SY22 6RE
GOLDEN LION - Tel: 01691 830295. Accommodation available. SY22 6RB

Shopping
SPAR shop with post office counter (Tel: 01691 831261) stays open until 10pm daily.

Connections
BUSES - as per Llanymynech.

Arddleen — Map 34

This roadside village (whose name means 'flax-garden') currently marks the end of navigation north of Welshpool.
THE HORSESHOE - Tel: 01938 590690. SY22 6PU
BUSES - as per Llanymynech.

BURGEDIN Locks were reopened in the summer of 1998. Above the locks, where a reedy backwater is all that remains of the Guilsfield Arm, you can only navigate for a mile or so to the flattened A483 bridge at Arddleen, but southwards some eleven miles of navigable canal stretch entertainingly as far as Bridge 129 beyond Berriew. The locks drop the canal by sixteen and a half feet to the sump level of the canal, making the Montgomery a peculiarity in a world where most man-made navigations climb up to, and descend from, a central summit.

At The Wern there is a slipway, winding hole and picnic area; the latter on the site of a former corn mill which derived its power from the sump level's plentiful supply of excess water produced by boats using the locks in either direction.

Southwards from The Wern the canal rides along an embankment above marshy ground, a remnant of the swamp which surrounded the Severn before it was drained early in the 19th century. On the far side of the river stand the Breidden Hills, seldom out of sight since you left Frankton. Now you can enjoy them in detail: quarry-scarred Breidden Hill itself, the most northerly summit, topped by a monument to Admiral Rodney by way of thanks for using Montgomeryshire timber in the building of his navy; and Moel y Golfa to the south with a memorial to Ernest Burton, King of Romanys. In a curious echo of the 18th Century naval memorial, the locality played host to a clandestine radio station built during the Second World War to enable the Admiralty to keep track of its vessels. Dominated by a trio of Eiffel Tower-shaped, seven hundred foot high masts (originally earmarked for erection in Ceylon!), the site continued to be strategically significant throughout the Cold War and into the 21st Century as a means of communicating with Britain's nuclear submarine fleet. The station closed and the masts were demolished in 2003.

Bank Lock is the first (or last) of four in close proximity which raise (or lower) the canal by some 35 feet. Each chamber has its segmented ground paddles, though these are not in general use. Crowther Hall Lock is the deepest on the canal. The charming lock cottage is

Breidden Hills

A483

Crse of Cambrian Railways
Oswestry-Welshpool

The Wern

Burgedin
Locks
16ft 6ins

P

slipway

B4392 to Guilsfield

Bank Lock
8ft 6ins
Pool Quay
(closed 1965)

SW/
ODP

St. John's
mp

Powis
Arms

River Severn

Severn Way
Offa's Dyke Path

site of
Strata
Marcella

Cabin
Lock
8ft 9ins

Crowther
Hall Lock
9ft 2ins

Pool Quay
Lock
8ft 9ins

The towpath south of Pool Quay is well used, as it forms both part of the Offa's Dyke Path (Chepstow-Prestatyn) and the Severn Way (Plynlimon-Bristol Channel), but north of Pool Quay it is unsurfaced and can become somewhat overgrown in summer; hardly impassable, but watch out for nettles and brambles if you're wearing shorts.

available for holiday lets. Down the adjoining lane is Crowther Hall, a handsome half-timbered farmhouse. Pool Quay's delightful Victorian church, with its elaborate and distinctively carved timber belfry, overlooks the next pound.

Pool Quay marked the head of navigation on the River Severn. It was, as the name suggests, the port, or quay, for Poole, an earlier name for Welshpool; though previously the settlement, the site of a notable Cistercian monastery, was known as Strata Marcella. The monks brought industry to the banks of the Severn and harnessed the river's power to drive a flour mill, textile works and forge. The Severn could only be navigated this far upstream in winter when there was sufficient depth of water, and with the advent of canal and railway transportation, carrying on the river had ceased by the mid 19th century. The railway, part of the Cambrian system absorbed by the Great Western, sadly closed in 1965, being part of the same route from Whitchurch to Welshpool whose ghost is encountered at various points along the Llangollen Canal. One of the station masters at Pool Quay was a bee-keeper who won prizes for his honey.

South of Pool Quay, Long Mountain assumes the vertical mantle of the Breiddens. Deep in its trench - unless sufficient rain has fallen on the hills of mid-Wales to make it break its banks - the Severn snakes about its valley floor, a modest watercourse difficult to associate with the broad navigable river of Gloucestershire featured in our *Severn & Avon Companion*. Briefly eluding the A483, the canal hides under the protective, wooded skirts of Yr Allt - a delightful stretch of waterway.

Crowther Hall Lock

Pool Quay   Map 35

Severnside settlement of considerable antiquity. Mid-nineteenth century maps depict a barytes grinding mill, corn mill, sawmill, flannel factory, blacksmiths and malt house with drying kilns. Now solely the relentless traffic on the A483 destroys the inherent calm of this lost inland port.

Eating & Drinking

THE POWIS ARMS - Tel: 01938 590255. Former coaching inn much refurbished after a period in the wilderness. Inglenook, real ale, home cooked food and accommodation. SY21 9JS *Morning coffees, light lunches and afternoon teas are enterprisingly served in the atmospheric precincts of St John's church on Thursdays, Fridays and Saturdays from Easter to the end of September.* Tel: 01938 590218.

Holiday Lets

CROWTHER HALL LOCK COTTAGE - Tel: 01938 590543. *www.canalcottageholidays.co.uk* Three bedroomed self-catering accommodation. Quarry-tiled floors, wood-burning stove and exposed beams but no telephone or television. Sounds heavenly! SY21 9JU

BUTTINGTON Wharf was an early development under the Montgomery Canal restoration programme and was home to the *Heulwen Sunshine*, a specially built trip boat for the handicapped which pioneered navigation on this length of canal from 1976. The wharf, popular with local people, has picnic tables and a trio of preserved limekilns, burnt lime having been widely used as an agricultural fertilizer before the introduction of chemicals. *Heulwen-Sunshine*, and her later sister vessel *Heulwen II*, now have a new base however, at the more recently constructed wharf by Bridge 116.

Road schemes seldom benefit canals. You only have to look as far as the Montgomery's flattened bridges to see the truth of this. Yet, paradoxically, the Welshpool by-pass twice came to the rescue of the town's canal: initially in 1969 when it was proposed to route the new road along the bed of the long moribund waterway, the threat of its loss crystallising a latent enthusiasm for the canal; then again in 1992/3 when the by-pass was finally constructed along a different course, allowing the previously flattened Gallows Tree Bank Bridge (No. 117) to be rebuilt with headroom for boats. Final completion of the by-pass and subsequent rebuilding of Whitehouse Bridge (No. 120) has resulted in the release of a dozen or so miles of navigable waterway.

Bungalows with neat gardens and Victorian villas - one with a monkey puzzle tree and a gazebo - herald the approach to Welshpool. Officially opened by Prince Charles in 1983, Welshpool Wharf is located south of Bridge 118 and incorporates a large mooring basin and slipway. Relatively little used at present, it is expected to be a valuable amenity when Montgomery Canal trade 'takes off'. The next (un-numbered) bridge, a metal girder structure, once carried the celebrated Welshpool & Llanfair Light Railway across the canal to its transhipment sidings by the standard gauge Cambrian Railways station, a flamboyant 'French chateau' style building now restored and open as a shopping complex. Eight miles of the 2ft 6ins gauge line pass through delightful countryside from Welshpool's Raven Square station to the rural terminus of Llanfair Caereinion.

Immediately south of the old railway bridge a small aqueduct, dated 1836, carries the canal over Lledan Brook. The semi-circular weir was part of a scheme whereby water was extracted by a local mill.

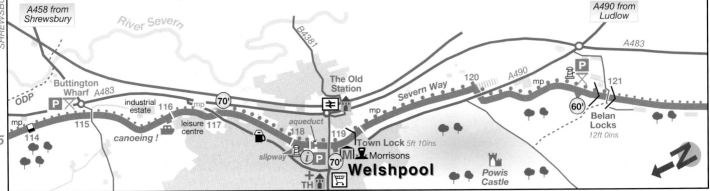

Welshpool's canalscape is quite delightful, the heart being centred on the old canal yard with its imposing and photogenic warehouse and adjoining cottages. The warehouse now serves as a local museum, though sadly the trip and hire boat operations formerly established are no longer a feature of the basin. Interestingly, archive photographs reveal that the overflow from Town Lock provided power for the water wheel of an adjoining corn mill.

Beyond the lock, the canal effects its exit from Welshpool rapidly, the urban environs being exchanged for sports grounds, housing and, before long, the gracious landscape of Powis Castle's parkland. A right angled turn takes the canal under Bridge 120 - no longer a barrier to navigation - and along a short new section of canal, wide and deep compared to the original course which is still in water and well utilised for fishing.

Belan Locks soon follow, raising the level of the canal by a total of twelve feet. Close by the lock cottage, with its neatly kept garden, is a group of amazingly ornate black and white cottages, occupied in bygone days by agricultural workers. On the horizon the green hills of Mid Wales enticingly beckon the southbound traveller onwards. But pause for a moment, turn and enjoy again the most splendid view of the Breidden Hills. Sometimes, it seems, the landscape - like life itself - is even better when looking back.

Welshpool (Y Trallwng)　　　Map 36

Monday is the day to immerse yourself in Welshpool when, as well as the general market, the weekly sheep and cattle market makes its colourful presence felt in the Smithfield alongside the canal. Down from the hills, farming folk congregate in the town to buy and sell, and to assuage the loneliness of their isolated lives in the freemasonry of the auction ring. And all day the town's pubs hum to the sing-song accents of Mid Wales, whilst the steeply climbing High Street, relatively quiet on other days, reverberates to the passage of cattle lorries, Landrovers and battered old cars plastered in the mud and slurry of far-flung farms.

Eating & Drinking

ROYAL OAK HOTEL - Severn Street. Tel: 01938 552217. Imposing hotel offering bar and restaurant food for non-residents. Local Welsh beers usually on tap. SY21 7DG

OLD STATION RESTAURANT - Old Station. Tel: 01938 556622. SY21 7AY

SPICE UK - Berriew Street. Tel: 01938 553431. Contempary Indian restaurant and take-away. SY21 7SQ

ANDREWS - High Street. Tel: 01938 552635. Award-winning fish & chips. SY21 7JP

Shopping

Good facilities for a relatively small town reflect Welshpool's importance as a centre for a wide agricultural hinterland. W. H. Smith, Somerfield, Sainsbury's and Boots constitute the usual suspects and their ilk, but there are plenty of local retailers too, such as Langford's butchers and food hall on Berriew Street, or Rikki Lloyd's butchers on High Street who've won prizes for their steak and kidney pies. There's a useful launderette adjacent to the imposing Victorian Town Hall on High Street and Brooks bicycle shop on Severn Street near the canal wharf. There are food markets on Mondays and Saturdays centred on the Town Hall and Broad Street. Morrisons supermarket beside Town Lock.

Things to Do

TOURIST INFORMATION CENTRE - Vicarage Garden Car Park (adjoining Bridge 118). Tel: 01938 552043. SY21 7DD

POWYSLAND MUSEUM - Canal Wharf. Tel: 01938 554656. Local history in the restored canal warehouse. Admission charge. SY21 7AQ

CLASSIC BUS SERVICE - Tel: 01691 780212. Round-trip of local sights operated in a vintage vehicle by Tanat Valley in conjunction with W'pool Town Council.

THE OLD STATION - Severn Road. Tel: 01938 556622. Conglomerate of specialist outlets housed in handsome former station building. Lots to keep the distaff side happy while the male of the species enjoys train sounds and railwayana. SY21 7AY

POWIS CASTLE, MUSEUM & GARDEN - Tel: 01938 551929. Famous garden, medieval castle and Clive Museum displaying treasures from India including textiles, armour, bronzes, jade, ivory etc. National Trust shop and licensed tea room. Admission charge. SY21 8RF

WELSHPOOL & LLANFAIR RAILWAY - Tel: 01938 810441. One of the 'Great Little Trains of Wales'. Services operate weekends April to late September, plus half term weekends in October; daily during summer holidays. Departures from Raven Square station at western edge of town approximately 20 minutes walk from the canal.

Connections

BUSES - services to/from Shrewsbury, Oswestry and Mid Wales. Tel: 0871 200 2233.

TRAINS - Arriva Trains Wales services to/from Shrewsbury, Newtown and the Cambrian Coast. Tel: 08457 484950.

TAXIS - Ambercars. Tel: 01938 556611. Castle Cabs. Tel: 01938 555343.

CALLOW Hill, at 1,247 feet, dominates the skyline to the south-east, part of the wonderful Shropshire hill country in the vicinity of Bishop's Castle. Brithdir Lock occupies a most delightful setting, its by-pass weir forming a pond-like feature beside a well-kept lawn. A copse of oak, ash and copper beech trees, set on an almost perfectly-rounded hill, provides an exquisite backdrop.

After climbing almost eight and a half feet through Berriew Lock, the canal is carried on an embankment across the Rhiw Valley and on to Berriew Aqueduct. An 1889 rebuild in brick of an earlier stone structure, the four-arched aqueduct (two river and two land arches) takes the waterway over the fast flowing waters of the Rhiw and the minor road into Berriew.

Flattened Bridge 129, carrying the B4385 road to Berriew, brings to an end the eleven mile navigable section down from Burgedin Locks. Financial constraints meant that construction of the Montgomeryshire Canal stalled in 1797 and for over twenty years Garthmyl, just over 16 miles from Carreghofa, was its terminus. What came to be known as the Western Branch through to Newtown was not completed until 1821. At Garthmyl was concentrated a series of wharves, warehouses, maltings, coal yards, stables and limekilns, and in its heyday the village must have been the scene of intense activity. It still is, but only from cars and lorries thundering along the A483, the widening of which in the 1940s obliterated most of the wharf area, although the old maltings are still in evidence beside an infilled section of canal. Garthmyl is also notable in that it is the closest point on the canal to Montgomery - just three miles away along the B4385. The county town was never an important commercial centre, however, and generated little trade for the canal.

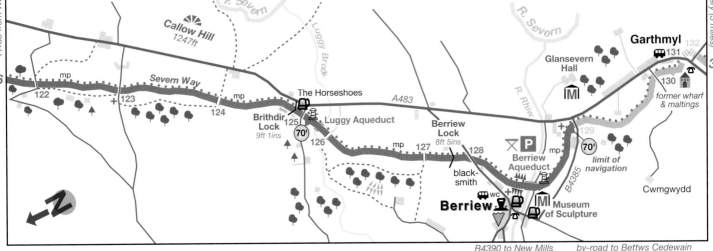

Berriew

Map 37

Enchanting village beside the River Rhiw, with clusters of black and white cottages huddling around the church and a handsome 18th century single span stone bridge. Good walking country.

Eating & Drinking

THE HORSESHOES - on A483 by Bridge 125. Tel: 01686 640282. Comfortably refurbished country pub. Garden (with lime kilns) and good choice of food. SY21 8AW

LION HOTEL - village centre. Tel: 01686 640452. Les Routiers recommended half-timbered inn offering accommodation, restaurant and bar meals. SY21 8PQ

THE TALBOT - Tel: 01686 64088. Comfortable small hotel idyllically located beside the River Rhiw. SY21 8PJ

Shopping

Spar supermarket, post office stores, butchers and gift shop.

Things to Do

WILLIAM O'BRIEN - Berriew Wharf. Tel: 01686 640739. Artist blacksmith occupying former canal warehouses. SY21 8AW

SILVER SCENES - Tel: 01686 640695. Silver plated giftware, showroom and factory outlet. Small charge for factory tours. SY21 8QA

ANDREW LOGAN MUSEUM OF SCULPTURE - beside the river. Tel: 01686 640689. A 'glittering, sparkling, fantasy wonderland' founded by the originator of the Alternative Miss World contest. Shop selling jewellery and sculpture. Mostly only open summer weekends. SY21 8AH

GLANSEVERN HALL - Tel: 01686 640200. 18 acres of garden in grounds of Greek Revival house on banks of the Severn. Open May-Sep, Thur, Fri, Sat & Bank Hol Mon afternoons. SY21 8AH

Horse Boating on the Monty

Robin Smithett

Connections

BUSES - Tanat Valley Coaches operate bi-hourly services Mon-Sat, to/from Newtown and Welshpool. Tel: 0871 200 2233.

Abermule

Map 38

Expanding village at the confluence of the Mule and Severn. A lovely cast iron bridge spans the Severn adjacent to canal Bridge 147. Large characters carry the inscription: 'THIS SECOND IRON BRIDGE CONSTRUCTED IN THE COUNTY OF MONTGOMERYSHIRE IN THE YEAR 1852'.

Eating & Drinking

ABERMULE HOTEL - village centre. Tel: 01686 630676. Small family run hotel frequented by fishermen; carvanners and campers also catered for. SY15 6ND

WATERLOO ARMS - village centre. Tel: 01686 630133. Home cooked food and real ales. SY15 6ND

Shopping

Village stores with post office counter ('saved' by Lembit Opik!). Tel: 01686 630201

Connections

BUSES - Tanat Valley Coaches operate bi-hourly services Mon-Sat, to/from Newtown and Welshpool. Tel: 0871 200 2233.

SURPRISINGLY deep and clear, the Monty meanders contentedly along the Severn Valley, the river and the A483 its constant companions: 'the towpath, in default of one along the Severn, is the pleasantest and easiest walk along the valley' wrote Brian Waters, the poet and topographical writer in *Severn Stream* published in 1949, and half a century has happily done nothing to make one argue with his view; indeed, the towpath has become officially adopted as the route of the Severn Way between Pool Quay and Newtown.

Two more flattened bridges, either side of the roadside hamlet of Fron, provide a stark reminder of the difficulties facing the return of full navigable status, portable boaters, however, can enjoy a rewarding sense of isolation. William Pugh, one of the prime movers in the canal's extension westwards, was born at Pennant. Wealthy, educated, and philanthropic, he built the Flannel Exchange in Newtown and put so much money into the canal and the local economy that he was forced to flee across the Channel to escape his creditors, dying a pauper's exile in 1842. The creditors may have been confounded, but retrospectively we can thank Pugh for this ravishingly beautiful canal.

By Bridge 140 you suddenly encounter a most lifelike wooden sculpture of a working boatman. At Brynderwen Lock the towpath briefly changes sides to accommodate a former coal wharf. Between Brynderwen and Byles locks, the A483 crosses the canal again before finally moving to the other side of the valley in the vicinity of Abermule; thereafter the canal is left in peace for the remainder of the journey to Newtown.

Abermule is remembered for being the site of a railway accident in 1921 when two trains - an Aberystwyth-Manchester express and a Whitchurch-Aberystwyth stopping train - collided head on along a stretch of single track; 17 people were killed and 36 injured. A happier railway memory is of the branchline from Abermule which threaded the gorge of the River Mule to the famous sheep-rearing centre of Kerry. Closed in 1956, in its final days the cattle trains, hauled by ancient 'Dean Goods', struggled up the grass-grown line solely to serve the monthly sheep fairs.

SHREWSBURY

ABERYSTWYTH

Abermule (closed 1965)

Abermule

Abermule Bridge

mp

B4386

148

Byles Lock
7ft 2ins

39

147

145 146

Severn Way

Brynderwen Lock
8ft 6ins

144

143

A483

River Severn

nature reserve

142

141

boatman statue

Fron

137 138 139 140

136

135

134

133

37

B4385

Pennant

The towpath is generally in good condition for walkers, though vegetation can reduce its width in places at the height of summer. *Severn Way* walkers seem few and far between.

for details of facilities at Abermule turn back to page 71

NEWHOUSE LOCK was restored in 2006. Slates in English and Welsh record that the opening ceremony was performed by Lembit Opik MP, though whether or not the Cheeky Girls were in attendance has not been recorded for posterity. A pair of idyllic houses overlooks the upper pound, one of their fortunate owners displays the perspicacity to keep a dinghy.

Bechan Brook is crossed on a three arched aqueduct before Bridge 152 carries the B4389 road into the hamlet of Aberbechan, the last settlement of any sort before Newtown. Paradoxically the towpath becomes surfaced as the canal becomes dry. Freestone Lock is derelict and gateless, the canal bed beyond a mass of rushes. Access is obtainable to Pwll Penarth Nature Reserve. The Severn broadens and Penarth Weir becomes audible, seeming to tease the moribund canal's inactivity. The weir was constructed by the canal's engineers in 1819 to convey water from the river into the canal. A cast iron sign reminds us that this was once the property of the Shropshire Union Railways & Canal Company.

Barely discernible, Dolfor Lock stands alongside a large sewage works. The Shropshire Union Canal Society have

relaid the hedge here, full restoration may be a pipe dream but small contributions like this are still worthwhile. The canal as such vanishes, but its course may be followed along a well defined pathway. Whether boats will ever come this way again remains to be seen, but for the time being it is enjoyable enough to be able to proceed on foot towards Newtown, accompanied perhaps by cyclists on National Route 81 which connects Shrewsbury with Aberystwyth.

As the Montgomery Canal nears its terminus there is no obvious clue as to the site of Rock Lock, the most westerly on the canal. An old pumping house which drew water for the canal up from the River Severn restores your faith that there was indeed a waterway here once. Together with an adjoining cottage and a cast iron overbridge, it looks more like a former railway station. Briefly the course of the canal runs at the rear of terraced houses, but beyond this point the canal has been built over and it is necessary to follow the riverside Severn Way into the centre of Newtown.

Should this abrupt end appear an anti-climax after the thirty-five mile journey from Welsh Frankton, consider instead the heady days of the nineteenth century when the area was a veritable hive of industry, a cornucopia of limekilns, foundries, coal and timber wharves. No less than seven dock arms extended from the the main basin, each

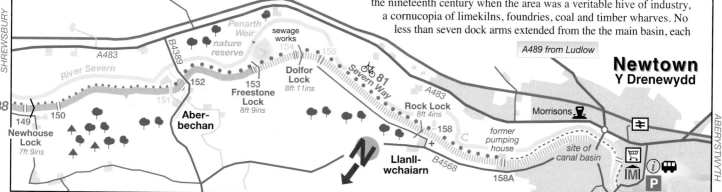

for details of facilities at Newtown turn to page 74

73

capable of holding two narrowboats simultaneously. By the twentieth century Newtown's mills were mainly mechanised and, whilst some used water power, others were steam operated and received their coal by canal. The last to do so were the Commercial Mills of Jones, Evans & Co, manufacturers of blankets, shawls and knitted goods. When they closed in 1935, they were still using 20 tons of coal a week. Mined in the collieries at Chirk, it was delivered by Tom Moody in his narrow boat *Endeavour*. Bearing in mind the ever deteriorating state of the Montgomery Canal, the round trip from Chirk probably took around a week to complete and it is doubtful whether he was able to carry any other traffic. When Jones, Evans & Co closed in 1935, Tom Moody stopped work, leaving George Beck as the last surviving boatman on the canal, until the breach of the following year put him out of business too.

Newtown (Y Drenewydd)   Map 39

Charm oozes from almost every non-porous brick in this mid-Wales market town whose longevity belies its name. Edward I granted the town a charter in 1279 but it was not until the nineteenth century that Newtown grew significantly with development of the woollen industry - at its zenith it acquired the sobriquet 'The Leeds of Wales'. Newtown's most famous son was Robert Owen (1771-1858), the successful capitalist whose socialist ideals inspired the Co-operative movement. His statue stands in Shortbridge Street and his tomb in the grounds of St Mary's ruined riverside church. Prominent on the southern edge of the town by the railway station is the Royal Welsh Warehouse. Erected by Pryce Pryce-Jones, a local draper, it is thought to have been the first mail order business in the world, numbering amongst its customers, Florence Nightingale and Queen Victoria. Pryce-Jones patented the Euklisia Rug, a forerunner of the sleeping bag and is credited with the concept of the parcel post. Another fine feature of this most likeable town is the plethora of impressive nonconformist chapels.

Accommodation
YESTERDAYS - Severn Street. Tel: 01686 622644. Superior guest house accommodation for the benefit of tired walkers. Huge Welsh breakfasts. SY16 2AG

Eating & Drinking
BANK COTTAGE TEA ROOMS - Shortbridge Street. Tel: 01686 625771. Everything a tea room ought to be. On clement days you can sit outside on the front patio eavesdropping on the eager gossip of lilting Welsh ladies and gazing down the street to the green hills beyond the gaunt warehouses and showrooms of Pryce-Jones. SY16 2AB
DRAGONS LAIR - Severn Street. Tel: 01686 624944. Cantonese restaurant. SY16 2AQ
JARMAN'S FISH RESTAURANT - High Street. Filling fish suppers for hungry walkers. Tel: 01686 625505. SY16 2NX
RAILWAY TAVERN - Old Kerry Road. Tel: 01686 626156. Convivial local on the way up to the railway station should you feel the need to reward yourself with a pint after a fifteen mile slog from Welshpool. SY16 1BH

Shopping
Chain stores lurk in the Bear Lanes Precinct off High Street and in Ladywell Shopping Centre off Shortbridge Street. Pearsonites are more discerning and make for the charming indoor market (Tuesday, Thursday, Friday and Saturday) or the launderette on Severn Street should all this walking have rendered them embarrassingly dishevelled.

Things to Do
TOURIST INFORMATION CENTRE - Central Car Park. Tel: 01686 625580. *www.newtown.org.uk* SY16 2PW
ROBERT OWEN MUSEUM - The Cross, Broad Street. Tel: 01686 626345. Museum (housed in glorious Arts & Crafts 'confection' of a building) telling the remarkable story of the man who inspired the Co-operative movement. Admission free. Open Mon-Sat throughout the year. SY16 2BB
W. H. SMITH MUSEUM - High Street. Tel: 01686 626280. The shop has been restored to its original state at the time it was first opened in 1927 and on the first floor is a fascinating small museum, highlighting many aspects of the company's business and tradition easily overlooked. Admission free. Open shop hours. SY16 2NP
TEXTILE MUSEUM - Commercial Street. On north bank of the Severn, enquire locally as to seasonal opening times.

Connections
BUSES - Arriva Cymru services to/from Welshpool and Shrewsbury with useful stops at Abermule and Berriew for shorter towpath walks. Tel: 0871 200 2233.
TRAINS - Arriva Trains Wales services to/from Welshpool, Shrewsbury and the Mid-Wales coast. Tel: 08457 484950.
TAXIS - Station Cabs. Tel: 01686 621818.

The Monmouthshire & Brecon Canal

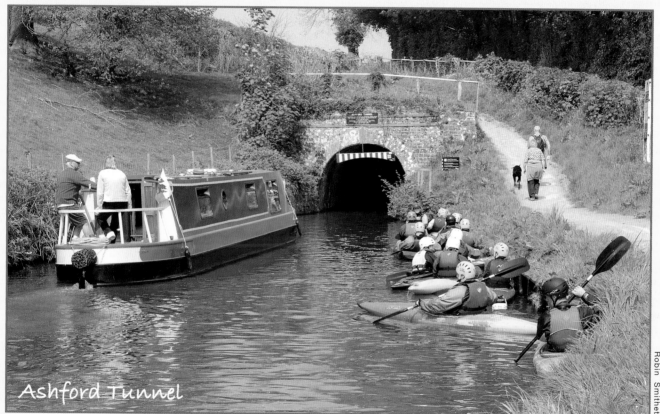

Ashford Tunnel

Robin Smithett

THE Monmouthshire Canal and the Brecon & Abergavenny Canal were built as two separate waterways. The former, opened in 1799, ran for eleven miles from the Usk Estuary at Newport to Pontnewynydd, north-west of Pontypool, with an eleven mile branch from Malpas to Crumlin; the latter, opened throughout in 1812, linked Brecon with Pontymoile, junction with the Monmouthshire, a distance of some 33 miles. In 1865 the Brecon & Abergavenny Canal was bought by the Monmouthshire Company, with the joint concern being taken over by the Great Western Railway in 1880. Commercial trade ended in the 1930s and the Monmouthshire Canal was largely abandoned, but the Brecon & Abergavenny Canal survived, primarily as a water feeder. With financial support from Monmouthshire and Brecon County Councils, the waterway was restored for navigation by British Waterways and reopened between Brecon and Pontymoile in 1970.

Subsequent restoration work has seen the limit of navigation pushed south as far as Five Locks, Cwmbran. Further proposals exist to restore the Mon & Brec all the way down to Newport and thus provide a link with the rest of the inland waterway network by way of the Usk and Severn estuaries. But for the time being navigability begins, or ends, at Five Locks, where a lowered road bridge and a flight of derelict locks bar any further progress south. A mooring basin and winding point have been provided and the surroundings are pleasant, if suburban, and a charming wooden sculpture of a narrowboat graces the presently infilled chamber of the top lock.

Inky and weedy and pea soup green with algae, the canal water betrays a prevalent hesitancy amongst boaters to venture south of Pontymoile. True, some may find the post-industrial communities of Pontnewydd, Sebastopol (which gained its name from the Crimean War) and Griffithstown too dour for their holiday-making sensibilities, but this is the *real* South Wales, an urban landscape of terraced houses and telegraph poles and time standing, apparently if not statistically, still. There is much to look out for and admire: Cwmbran

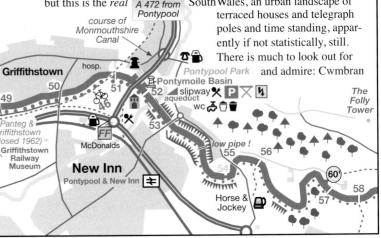

Tunnel - just 87 yards long with a path over the top - lies cradled in a bower of green open space separating Pontnewydd from Sebastopol and by its northern portal a surviving Monmouthshire Canal milepost informs that the Newport terminus of the canal lies 7 miles to the south; converted into National Cycle Route No.46, the trackbed of the Newport & Blaenavon Railway crosses the canal on high, skewed girders by Bridge 51; nearby a museum celebrates (amongst myriad other railway matters) that the Associated Society of Locomotive Engineers and Firemen was formed here in 1880; the rather forbidding hospital bordering the offside of the canal between bridges 50 and 51, was originally the Pontypool Poor Law Institution.

Pontymoile Basin marks the former junction of the Monmouthshire and Brecon & Abergavenny canals. Nowadays it's a popular leisure asset for nearby Pontypool. A tearoom and picnic site draw the locals. Here, in the canal's working past, boats were assessed for tolls as they went from one canal to the other. Close by, an aqueduct - the tallest on the Mon & Brec - carries the canal over the Afon Llwyd.

Narrowboat sculpture - Pontnewydd

Summary of Facilities
Eating & Drinking
OPEN HEARTH - canalside between bridges 48 & 49. Tel: 01495 763752. A tradition of steel-making gives this friendly canalside pub (and *Good Beer Guide* fixture) its curious name. Real ales and a wide-ranging menu make this probably the best port of call in the vicinity. NP4 5DR

HORSE & JOCKEY - east of Bridge 55. Tel: 01495 762721. Pretty thatched pub with easy reach of the canal. Nice garden. NP4 0JB

PAGES FISH BAR - Bridge 48. Tel: 01495 753185. Reputedly one of the best in South Wales! NP4 5BQ

Also: floating tea bar at Pontymoile Basin, a McDonalds drive-thru and Harvester restaurant overlooking the roundabout east of Pontymoile Basin once occupied by 86G - Pontypool Road railway engine shed!

Shopping
It is advisable that you lay in stores higher up the canal, for along this lower navigable length - other than trekking into Pontypool or Cwmbran - one has to rely on the meagre stocks of corner shops for victualling the galley.

Things to Do
GRIFFITHSTOWN RAILWAY MUSEUM - Station Road, Griffithstown (east of Bridge 49). Tel: 01495 762908. Former Great Western Railway goods shed housing a nostalgic collection of railwayana recalling the great days of 'God's Wonderful Railway' generally, and the dense railway network of the local area specifically. Also celebrates Charles Perry, founder of ASLEF. Model railway shop. Open daily, small admission fee, refreshments. NP4 5JH

Connections
BUSES - services to/from Newport from stops by Bridge 48. Tel: 0871 200 2233.

TRAINS - stations at Cwmbran and Pontypool & New Inn offer links with the outside world and the possibility of one-way towpath walks to/from Abergavenny. Tel: 08457 484950.

TAXIS - A Class. Tel: 01495 759490.

UTPOSTS of industry - fibre and pharmaceutical plants - pepper the valley, but up in its hillside setting, the canal remains tree-lined and secretive, demarcating the boundaries of traditional hill farms, like the picturesquely whitewashed one between bridges 75 and 76 with the monkey puzzle tree in its small garden. Look out also for the peculiar house by Bridge 81 with an opening for a boat at water level. Goytre Wharf is one of the canal's showpieces, a preserved example of the kind of industrial facility which flourished in the canal's commercial heyday with arms and a rank of limekilns.

This stretch of the canal features in Alexander Cordell's historical saga *Rape of the Fair Country* in which he writes vividly of lying on the prow of a barge watching the water-lilies and bindweed waving as sunlight streams through the trees casting golden patterns on the boat. Another of his books - widely available locally - called *Song of the Earth* is set on the Neath & Tennant Canals.

Mamhilad
STAR INN - adjacent Bridge 62. Tel: 01495 785319. Re-opened gastro-pub. NP4 0JF
HORSESHOE INN - quarter of a mile north of Bridge 65. Tel: 01873 880542. Another comfortable country inn. NP4 0JB

Goytre Wharf
WATERSIDE RESTAURANT - Tel: 01873 881355. Cafe/restaurant located at Goytre Wharf adjoining the Canal Centre. NP7 9EW
GOYTRE WHARF - canal heritage visitor centre. Tel: 01873 881069.

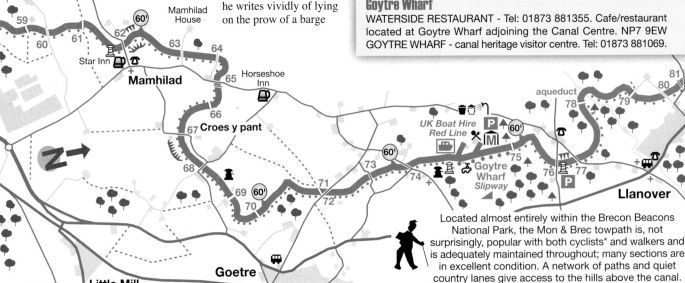

Located almost entirely within the Brecon Beacons National Park, the Mon & Brec towpath is, not surprisingly, popular with both cyclists* and walkers and is adequately maintained throughout; many sections are in excellent condition. A network of paths and quiet country lanes give access to the hills above the canal.

*British Waterways should be consulted as to along which sections of the towpath cycling is currently permitted.

Near Llanover

REQUENT occupation bridges - some humped, some flat-decked - punctuate the canal's progress along the 367 foot contour line above the valley of the Usk. Thomas Dadford Junior's feat of essaying a twenty-five mile pound in such mountainous surrounds is a remarkable achievement. Occasionally you find yourself wishing, uncharacteristically, that there were less trees, because they do tend to mask the views, so it is tempting to reach for your rucksack and take to the hills to do more justice to such splendid scenery. Between bridges 85 and 87, towpath walkers can shave a few hundred yards off the journey, by taking to a path through the woods. This path runs steeply down to cross a stream on a footbridge bearing a sign warning of the existence of a troll - see what you miss by keeping resolutely to the canal! Llanover House belonged to one Benjamin Hall, who, as Commissioner of Works, gave his name to London's most famous horological landmark, Big Ben.

Llanfoist Wharf is the home of Beacon Park Boats, surely one of the most beautifully-sited hire bases in the country. It may be difficult to imagine that this quiet place was once the scene of intense industrial activity. Hill's tramroad linked the ironworks at Blaenavon and forge at Garnddyrys with the canal wharf and the Llanvihangel tramroad on the valley floor below. To explore the route of the tramroad, go down the steps adjacent to Bridge 95A to reach the road and the entrance to the tunnel, which leads uphill beneath the canal to the tramroad incline. The route can be followed up the hillside and on to Blorenge Mountain whose 1,833ft summit can be reached in a couple of hours.

North of Llanfoist Wharf the canal skirts the edge of a beech wood and passes the imposing Llanfoist House, once the home of Crawshaw Bailey, the ironmaster of Nantyglo and MP for Monmouth. A major breach occurred at White House Turn in 1975, when thousands of gallons of water cascaded down onto parts of the village below the canal. Six years were to pass before the breach was repaired and the section reopened.

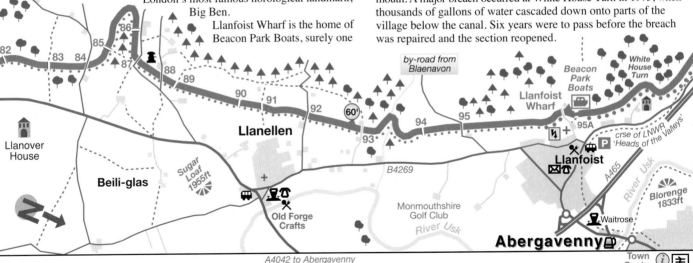

Llanellen
Map 42

Small village tucked below the canal on the busy Pontypool to Abergavenny main road. Village stores and Old Forge Crafts (Tel: 01873 854811 - NP7 9HT) which offers gifts and refreshments, *Welsh* teas being a speciality.

Llanfoist
Map 42

The remains of the ironmaster Crawshaw Bailey lie in the cemetery of the pretty little church of St Faith's (a 3rd Century martyr) which you pass on your steep descent from the canal. The village pub has been turned into an Asian restaurant and takeaway called EXOTIC EAST - Tel: 01873 850509. NP7 9LP Regular bus services operate to Abergavenny. Station Cars - Tel: 01873 857233 - provide a more personalised transport link.

Abergavenny
Map 42

Canallers may legitimately wish that Hamelin of Ballon had sited his 11th Century castle on the *west* bank of the Usk and that Abergavenny had subsequently developed much closer to where the canal was eventually dug. Similarly, railway enthusiasts may mourn the closure of the Heads of the Valleys line in 1958, prior to which they could have caught a local train at Govilon and passed triumphantly over the Usk into Abergavenny (Brecon Road) in a cloud of smoke and steam. Present day reality is more banal, and you will need to catch a bus or call a taxi, or make the mile long journey under your own steam. But make it one must, for it is well nigh impossible to resist the siren call of the town hall tower - positively Ruritanian in its lofty eminence - and the town itself, however one eventually reaches it - is of enormous appeal.

Eating & Drinking

ANGEL HOTEL - Cross Street. Tel: 01873 857121. Handsome coaching inn offering bar and restaurant food and accommodation. NP7 5EN

THE TRADING POST - Nevill Street. Tel: 01873 855448. Atmospheric coffee house and bistro. NP7 5AD

LAZY DAYS - Frogmore Street. Tel: 01873 855572. Bustling cafe offering a wide choice of fresh hot snacks.

MARKET STREET FISH & CHIPS - Market Street. Tel: 01873 855791. Classic fish & chips restaurant/take-away. NP7 5SD

COLISEUM - Lion Street. Tel: 01873 736960. Wetherspoon conversion of old cinema. NP7 5PE

KINGS ARMS - Nevill Street. Tel: 01873 855074. Gastro-pub and micro-brewery. Accommodation. NP7 5AA

LA BRASSERIE - Lewis's Lane. Tel: 01873 737937. Contemporary Italian. NP7 5AB

WALNUT TREE INN - Llanddewi Skirrid. Tel: 01873 852797. Fine dining at internationally famous restaurant three miles from Abergavenny. A taxi jaunt for the well-heeled hungry. NP7 8AW

Shopping

Quarter of an hour's walk from the canal, there's a WAITROSE supermarket. But it is Abergavenny's independent shops - like Rawlings the butchers on Market Street, and Edwards butcher and delicatessen on Flannel Street - that really contribute to the pleasure of shopping here. Look out too for Nicholls department store, the Abergavenny Book Shop on High Street and Abergavenny Music on Cross Street if you're a bookworm or music lover. The lively retail market which they're so proud of takes place on Tuesday in and around the handsome market hall. There are additional retail markets on Fridays and Saturdays, a fabulous Flea Market on Wednesdays and a Farmers Market on the fourth Thursday in the month. By the way, don't miss Burton's men's clothes shop retaining its 'Tailor of Taste' slogan and gold-leafed list of towns with branches. Abergavenny's growing reputation as a food centre culminates each September in a fabulous Food Festival. *www.abergavennyfoodfestival.com*

Things to Do

TOURIST INFORMATION - Swan Meadow, Monmouth Road. Tel: 01873 857588. *www.visitabergavenny.co.uk* NP7 5HH

ABERGAVENNY MUSEUM AND CASTLE - Castle Street. Tel: 01873 854282. Admission charge. Open daily March-October, closed Sundays November-February. Displays trace the history of the town from Roman times. NP7 5EE

SUGAR LOAF MOUNTAIN - Perhaps the finest - and not unduly difficult - walk in the area is to the 1,955ft summit of Sugar Loaf mountain. The view from the top will stay with you for ever! Advice on this and other walks from the TIC.

Connections

BUSES - services to/from Brecon, Cardiff, Pontypool, Cwmbran and Newport. Cardiff service calls at Llanfoist, Govilon and Gilwern; Brecon buses stop at Crickhowell and Talybont. Tel: 0871 200 2233.

TRAINS - Arriva Trains Wales services to/from Shrewsbury, Cwmbran and Newport. Tel: 08457 484950.

TAXIS - Station Cars. Tel: 01873 857233.

OVILON Wharf plays host to British Waterways Section Office, as well as to Govilon Boat Club. The wharf was once the terminus of the Llanvihangel tramroad, opened to Llanvihangel in 1814 and to Hereford in 1819. Closed in 1846, it subsequently became a railway, a branch line between Abergavenny and Merthyr. In *The Forgotten Railways of South Wales* (published by David & Charles in 1979) James Page opined this sadly abandoned railway line 'the most spectacular in South Wales'. Its passenger trains have gone but the station, just uphill from Bridge 98, has become a private home whilst the trackbed is now a footpath and cycleway. William Bliss alighted here with his canoe and baggage to begin his canoeing trip along the Mon & Brec Canal, as described in *Rapid Rivers*, published in 1935. He wrote of this section of the canal: 'I landed on the right bank and walked across the road, and then saw below me the Usk valley clothed in woods and the town of Abergavenny on the further side, and opposite to me the Sugar Loaf hill and behind that the great mass of the Black Mountains rising up to nearly three thousand feet. Then the canal made a bend to cross the little Llanwenarth brook, and between that and Gilwern there were wonderful open views from the canal itself up the Usk Valley. I was glad I had come. It was late May, and everything was green and happy and there was no-one there but me'.

Amazingly little has changed. There are still wonderful views up the Usk Valley and across to the Sugar Loaf and Black Mountains, and everything is still 'green and happy'. As for there being 'no-one there', well we can't promise that, but the Mon & Brec is considerably quieter than the main canal network. Govilon's parish church nestles snugly beneath the canal's embankment. It dates from the middle of the 19th Century, before which villagers crossed the Usk by ferry to pay their devotions. The lych-gate commemorates a former village schoolmaster who rejoiced in the euphonious name of Ivor Tossell. The canal has been re-routed at Bridge 101A as part of a road improvement scheme.

At Gilwern a right-angled bend takes the canal across the Clydach Gorge on a 90 foot high embankment. On the south side was the Clydach Iron Company's wharf, where the Llam-march tramroad brought down coal from the Llam-march mines and iron from the Clydach iron-works. Below the canal ran both the river and the Clydach Railroad, which went down to the Usk at Glangrwyney, a mile from Gilwern. Branches led to further wharves and to the Clydach Basin, now the hire base of Castle Narrowboats. Mooring facilities are provided on both sides of the aqueduct and paths and steps link the wharf, towpath and tramroad tunnel, allowing a thorough exploration of the area. Bridge 104, was the site of a number of limekilns and an old coal wharf, originally constructed by the Brecon Boat Company.

It was in the neighbourhood of Bridge 106 that a breach occurred in October 2007 which resulted in the canal being closed for over a year. Seven houses were evacuated and eight people rescued. Subsequently, sixteen miles of canal were closed for a geotechnical survey to be carried out and ninety leaks were discovered. A hundred thousand fish had to be relocated. In the end some £15 million was spent on refurbishing the canal, an outlay commensurate with the canal's annual contribution to the local economy. The canal bank between bridges 105 and 106 has been reinstated using environmentally-friendly materials planted with native species.

Govilon

Govilon   Map 43
The massive bulk of the Blorenge mountain looms over Govilon dominating the village as the Matterhorn dominates Zermatt. A romanticised analogy perhaps, but Govilon's setting is truly dramatic, especially in winter when the great hill is snow covered.
Eating & Drinking
BRIDGEND INN - Church Lane, best approached via the aqueduct steps. Tel: 01873 830177. *GBG* recommended pub serving a good choice of guest beers. Lunches, evening meals and a self-evident enthusiasm for folk music. NP7 9RP
LION INN - Main Street. Tel: 01873 830404. Village centre local. NP7 9PT
Shopping
VILLAGE STORES - Tel: 01873 830350. Open daily from 7.30 am through to 6.30pm (noon on Sundays). NP7 9PT
Connections
BUSES - sevice No.3 runs hourly, Mon-Sat, linking Govilon with Abergavenny and Brynmawr. X4 also runs hourly, Mon-Sat, linking Abergavenny with Cardiff via Govilon, Brynmawr, Ebbw Vale,

Tredegar, Merthyr Tydfil and Pontypridd. Tel: 0871 200 2233.

Gilwern   Map 43
Humdrum village in a wonderful setting - breathtaking views across the Usk Valley to the Black Mountains.
Eating & Drinking
BRIDGEND INN - canalside Bridge 103. Tel: 01873 830939. Felinfoel beers from Llanelli and a good choice of food. NP7 0AU
Fish & chips just down from Bridge 103 - Tel: 01873 832040.
Shopping
Post office, general store and pharmacy on road leading down from Bridge 103; SPAR shop in garage on A4077.
Connections
BUSES - sevice No.3 runs hourly, Mon-Sat, linking Gilwern with Abergavenny and Brynmawr. X4 also runs hourly, Mon-Sat, linking Abergavenny with Cardiff via Gilwern, Brynmawr, Ebbw Vale, Tredegar, Merthyr Tydfil and Pontypridd. Tel: 0871 200 2233.

Robin Smithett

83

A SPECTACULAR panorama greets the Brecon bound traveller emerging from the woods beyond Bridge 109. Glance behind at the Sugar Loaf; down to Crickhowell nestling beside the Usk against the dramatic backdrop of Table Mountain and the Black Mountains; and ahead to the imposing bulk of Mynydd Llangattock. Remember the passage through Llanfoist Wood and thinking that the scenery couldn't get any better? Perhaps it can after all. Try mooring for the night near Bridge 111, then, as daylight fades, watch the lights twinkling in the cottages and farms far across the valley, like a sea of stars in a cloudless sky. It was on this section, close by Bridge 110, that cutting of the canal began in April 1796.

Llangattock is the most obvious mooring point for a visit to the pleasant town of Crickhowell, a mile away across the Usk. On the way you cross Crickhowell Bridge which, in its present form, dates from 1810. From downstream it appears to have thirteen arches, from upstream only twelve!

There are limekilns at the wharf beyond Bridge 115; another tramroad route (Darren Cilau) leading up the Llangattock escarpment from Bridge 114; and an aqueduct over the Nant Onneu, a tributary of the Usk. And all around are the magnificent mountains. A stiff two hour climb, partly following the route of the tramroad, will take you to the summit of Mynydd Pen-cyrn (1,735 feet).

Bridge 118 is known as Workhouse Bridge, but the object of this haunting association has thankfully become an hospitable hotel. Amongst other events, Glanusk Park hosts the annual Green Man music festival. The estate was established in 1826 by Sir Joseph Bailey who, like his brother Crawshaw (see Map 42), had made his fortune in iron production. The original mansion was demolished after being set on fire by the Army, who had requisitioned it during the Second World War, but the imposing Dower House remains. In 1876 the estate's gamekeeper was shot dead whilst trying to apprehend poachers.

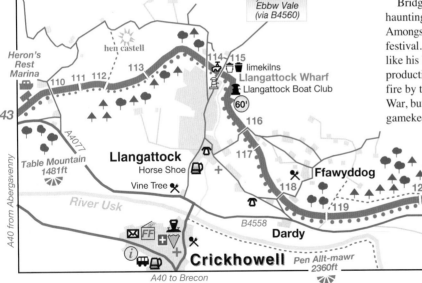

Llangattock

Map 44

Llangattock takes its name from the church of St Catwg, founded in the 6th century and rebuilt in the 12th. Tucked away down a narrow lane, the village stocks and whipping post are contained within its grounds. Dominated by the quarried face of the Llangattock escarpment, the village is a mix of modern bungalows and old cottages.

Eating & Drinking

HORSE SHOE INN - village centre. Tel: 01873 810393. Unspoilt country inn. Bar meals lunchtimes and evenings. NP8 1PA

THE VINE TREE - A4077. Tel: 01873 810514. Nicely appointed bar and restaurant overlooking Crickhowell Bridge, well worth the walk down from the canal. Breconshire Brewery beers. NP8 1HG

TY CROESO - just uphill from Bridge 118. Tel: 01873 810573. Hotel with restaurant open to non-residents Tue-Sun from 7pm; also for light lunches and teas during July and August. NP8 1PU

Crickhowell

Map 44

A delightful small town increasingly well known for its annual Walking Festival at the beginning of March. The name is the Anglicised form of Crug Hywel, the rampart and the ditch stronghold of Hywel Dda - now known as Table Mountain, which overlooks the town.

Eating & Drinking

BEAR HOTEL - High Street. Tel: 01873 810408. Immensely comfortable and welcoming 15th century coaching inn; all beams, big fireplaces and flagstones. Bar and restaurant meals plus very tempting accommodation. Winner of many awards! NP8 1BW

DRAGON INN - High Street. Tel: 01873 810362. Well appointed and atmospheric hotel and restaurant rivalling The Bear. NP8 1BE

Near Llangattock

Robin Smithett

NUMBER EIGHTEEN - High Street. Tel: 01873 812429. Contemporary cafe specialising in local organic ingredients open daily 9am-6pm.

Shopping

Shopping here is a pleasure, the emphasis being on characterful individual retail outlets such as ASKEWS BAKERY, CASHELLS and RICHARDS butchers shops, and WEBBS IRONMONGERS. BACCHUS, the appropriately named off-licence, stocks a thirst-inducing range of Welsh beers.

Things to Do

RESOURCE & INFORMATION CENTRE - Beaufort Street. Tel: 01873 811970. Fine new modern information centre with cafe. NP8 1BN

Connections

BUSES - service X43 connects Crickhowell approximately bi-hourly, Mon-Sat, with Brecon (via Llangynidr and Talybont) and Abergavenny. Tel: 0871 200 2233.

TAXIS - Crickhowell Taxis. Tel: 01873 811764.

T Llangynidr (difficult for the English to pronounce but try 'Llan-gun-idder') the 25 mile pound from Five Locks, Cwmbran finally comes to an end. It makes a pleasant change to have some locks to work and, like English wickets going down in a Test Match, you don't just get one or two, but five in quick succession. Designed - like most locks in South Wales - to accommodate boats of 63ft length and 8ft 6ins beam, they are spread over less than a mile and lift the canal up by 48 feet. Local practice is to leave the locks empty with bottom gates open; something of an inconvenience as it means you always have to fill the lock first when locking down, or empty it afterwards when locking up. But no-one should be in a hurry to work through the Llangynidr locks,

as it's difficult to think of a more gorgeous flight anywhere in Britain (perhaps only Bosley on the Macclesfield comes close). Between the first and second locks the canal crosses the River Crawnon on a sizeable aqueduct equipped with a plug and conventional windlass to drain this section of the canal. Public moorings are provided here, presenting the opportunity to be lulled to sleep by the babbling waters of the Crawnon. Above the second lock is the hire base of Country Craft, then the top three locks follow in quick succession, overlooked by the almost perfectly rounded summit of Tor y Foel.

A former workhouse - subsequently two agricultural workers' cottages - stands beside Bridge 136. Today it serves as a highly desirable private residence.

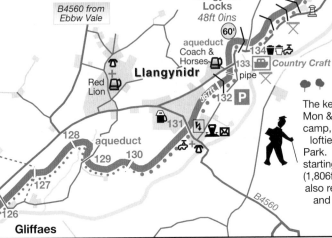

The keen hiker will rapidly realise that a boat on the Mon & Brec can be used as a kind of floating base camp, providing convenient access to many of the loftier summits in the Brecon Beacons National Park. Bridge 134, for example, represents a good starting point for the wonderful ascent of Tor y Foel (1,806ft). For a gentler walk from Llangynidr, we can also recommend the path that follows the Usk up and downstream from the B4560 road bridge.

A short stroll downhill from Bridge 138 stands the little Tudor church of St Tetta at Llandetty. Nearby a decrepit suspension bridge spans the Usk. It was probably erected to enable people from Buckland Hall to visit the church. Ashford Tunnel is 375 yards long with no towpath; in bygone days horses went over the top and boats were poled through. It was built as a 'dig and fill tunnel', whereby a cutting was first made and the tunnel built, then the earth was put back over the tunnel. Boaters need to exercise caution, as it is very narrow with low headroom, particularly towards the Llangynidr end. At the southern portal a plaque commemorates the fact that, after a period of closure for repair, the tunnel was officially reopened on 5th May 1985, the ceremony being performed by Mr Trevor Luckuck; his name is depicted in large capital letters. Mr Luckuck was, of course, British Waterways' Deputy Chief Executive at the time: oh for the immortality of petty officialdom!

Beyond the tunnel the B4558 runs alongside the canal but carries little traffic. Peace and tranquillity still rule the roost hereabouts.

Llanynidr   Map 45

Set in perhaps the most dramatic section of the Usk Valley, Llangynidr is undoubtedly one of the shiniest jewels in the Mon & Brec crown. The village comprises three distinct parts: Upper Llangynidr, half a mile from Bridge 129; Cwm Crawnon close to the 'Coach & Horses'; and Lower Llangynidr, also known as Coed-yr-ynys, which is down by the Usk. The latter is the most pleasing, an enchanting jumble of cottages close to the ancient and picturesque six-arched bridge over the river. The locals tell us that when the weather is hot, bathing from the flat rocks in the Usk is an experience not to be missed. Can you believe it's ever that warm? We can't, but we'll settle for enjoying the breathtaking views of the valley from Usk Bridge. Good at any time of the year, but most memorable in late October/early November.

Eating & Drinking

RED LION HOTEL - Upper Llangynidr. Tel: 01874 730223. Bar & restaurant meals plus bed & breakfast in this nice old inn near the church. NP8 1NT

COACH & HORSES - canalside Bridge 133. Tel: 01874 730245. Justifiably one of the most popular pubs on the Mon & Brec. Good choice of beers, bar and restaurant meals, accommodation and

Llangynidr

Robin Smithett

attractive canalside garden. NP8 1LS

Shopping

WALNUT TREE STORES, in Lower Llandgynidr, well-stocked village stores/newsagent/off-licence/post office. Tel: 01874 730309. NP8 1NA

Connections

BUSES - services to Brecon and Abergavenny via Crickhowell. Tel: 0871 200 22

Pencelli   Map 46

Shopless village on the B4558, but there is a snug little pub called the ROYAL OAK, (Tel: 01874 665396) a 300 year old inn featuring home-made food, canalside garden and a choice of locally-brewed real ales. LD3 7LX

Talybont-on-Usk   Map 46

Quiet holiday centre that relishes its position beside, or rather, below the canal which passes through the village on a substantial embankment. Visitors include cavers, abseilers and rock climbers as well as boaters.

Eating & Drinking

TRAVELLER'S REST - adjacent Bridge 142 (Map 45). Tel: 01874 676233. Well-appointed country inn with accommodation. LD3 7YP

WHITE HART - Bridge 143. Tel: 01874 676227. LD3 7JD

STAR INN - canalside by aqueduct. Tel: 01874 676635. *Good Beer Guide* entry with wide choice of beer and B & B. LD3 7YX

USK INN - Tel: 01874 676251. Comfortable accommodation and award-winning food at inn which opened to cater for the railway trade. LD3 7JE

Shopping

Well stocked post office stores also offering hot & cold snacks and carry-out teas and coffees for towpath walkers and others in need of sustenance. Tel: 01874 676663.

Connections

BUSES - service X43 runs bi-hourly, Mon-Sat, to/from Abergavenny and Brecon. Tel: 0871 200 2233.

XECUTING a nifty right angled turn, the Mon & Brec drifts across the Afon Caerfanell on a narrow aqueduct and into Talybont-on-Usk, focal point of the northern end of the canal. The village is one of the most popular ports of call on the canal, and you may encounter canoeists on the canal, mountain bikers on the towpath and hikers in the hills. Many people arriving here - ourselves included - find it hard to drag themselves away, so much is there to see and do, including exploration of the route of the old Bryn Oer Tramroad, which ran for twelve miles from the Bryn Oer colliery near Rhymney via the Trevil limestone quarry. It forms part of the Taff Trail, a long distance path from Cardiff to Brecon that continues along the towpath to the canal terminus. Running parallel to the tramroad is the line of the former Brecon & Newport Railway, which closed in 1962.

Talybont drawbridge was converted into a fixed structure in 1944,

thus preventing navigation to Brecon to all but canoes and very small boats. It was replaced by a wooden drawbridge in 1970 when the canal was reopened throughout. The present bridge is electrically powered.

A series of lift bridges follows, all hydraulically operated, before the canal passes through the moat of Pencelli Castle. Apart from the original mound, little remains of the once significant medieval castle, although Pencelli Castle farmhouse has taken both its name and some of its stone.

Take a deep breath - the most awe-inspiring section of this fabulous canal is just about to begin. Weather permitting, you'll get your first sight of flat-topped Pen y Fan, highest of the Brecon Beacons at 2,907 feet, a four hour (one way) climb from Bridge 158 via Llanfrynach. Even better views of the Beacons are to come at Bridge 160, beyond the marina and hire base of Cambrian Cruisers. Certainly this canal lives up to E. F. Schumacher's epithet - 'Small is Beautiful'.

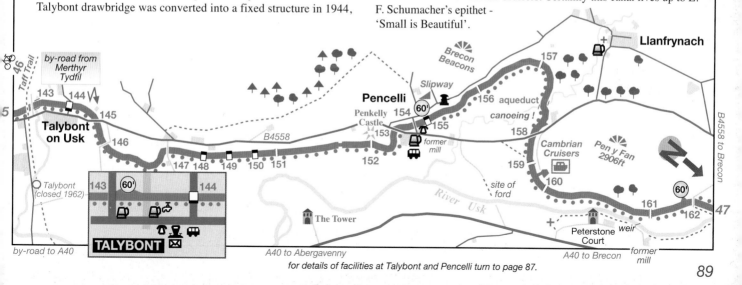

for details of facilities at Talybont and Pencelli turn to page 87.

THE canal reached Brecon in 1800. A couple of centuries later the canal still leaps powerfully across the River Usk on a substantial four arched stone aqueduct approached (from both directions) by a right angled bend. The water channel narrows to 12 feet for the length of the aqueduct, and at the south end an overflow weir takes away winter flood water. Extensive repairs were carried out on the aqueduct in 1996-97, during which mooring bollards were installed close to the overflow weir. This is a popular overnight stop, although noise from the nearby A40 road detracts slightly from its appeal. Incidentally, this A40 is the old road from London to Fishguard for the Irish ferry trade.

Now there's just the small matter of Brynich Lock to negotiate - lifting the canal up by ten feet to its summit level of 425 feet - and you're on the final stage of the journey to Brecon. Above the lock the water is deep and crystal clear; it's such a novelty for canal water to be so clean that you tend to stare transfixed over the side of the boat, expecting to see ... who knows what? We saw nothing, except several shoals of silvery fish and several shoals of silvery beer cans.

The Brecon Beacons make

their final appearance for a while, towering imperiously above the lesser hills that surround them.

The towpath here is part of National Cycle Route 8, otherwise known as Lon Las Cymru which runs all the way from Cardiff to Holyhead - a mere 250 miles! On the offside the B4601 road runs close alongside, but a thick belt of trees prevents traffic noise from becoming intrusive.

Until comparatively recently the canal voyage to Brecon ended with something of a whimper, as the waterway ground to a miserable halt in a wall beyond Gasworks Bridge. Gasworks Bridge! The name conjures up all sorts of images, none of which are appropriate to the Mon & Brec. But now the canal ends, if not with a bang, at least with a sizeable pop, at the terminal basin.

Passing under a new bridge, named after Thomas Dadford, the canal's engineer, you arrive in the basin which provides extensive moorings as well as a winding point. You can tie up in pleasant surroundings outside the Theatr Brycheiniog, the perfect place to reflect on your visit to the Monmouthshire & Brecon Canal, a waterway of immense beauty and unique, self-defining charm. The town of Brecon itself deserves a day or two of your attention, and then you can look forward to the joy of the journey back!

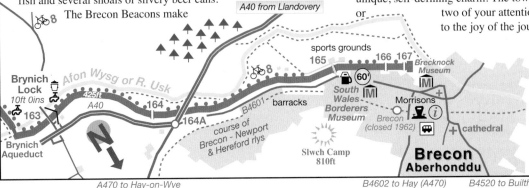

Market town, administrative centre for the Brecon Beacons National Park, seat of the diocese of Swansea and Brecon and mecca for walkers and climbers, Brecon is a friendly place; certainly no anti-climax at the end of a voyage up the Mon & Brec. The oldest part of town surrounds the castle remains near the confluence of the Usk and Honddu rivers. An attractive 'promenade' by the Usk, reached via Watergate, provides superb views of the Beacons. Every August, New Orleans comes to town with the staging of the internationally-renowned Brecon Jazz Festival. Every September the locally garrisoned Ghurkas go on parade. Dancing and marching: what better ways of passing time has man ever fallen upon?

Eating & Drinking

THE WELLINGTON HOTEL - The Bulwark. Tel: 01874 625225. Town centre hotel offering bar and restaurant food plus an 'authentic' French creperie called Eliza Blues. LD3 7AP
ROBERTO'S - St Mary Street. Tel: 01874 611880. Little Italian restaurant overlooked by St Mary's Church. LD3 7AA
TIPPLE 'N' TIFFIN - Canal Wharf. Tel: 01874 611866. Modern informal dining overlooking canal basin. LD3 7EW
PILGRIMS TEA ROOMS - Cathedral Close. Tel: 01874 610610. Open daily for coffees, lunches and teas with emphasis on traditional Welsh fare. LD3 9DP
BRECON BALTI - Glamorgan Street. Tel: 01874 624653. Restaurant and takeaway. LD3 7DW
BULL'S HEAD - The Street. Tel: 01874 623900. Evan Evan beers from Llandeilo, Carmarthenshire. LD3 7LS
OLD BOAR'S HEAD - Ship Street. Tel: 01874 622856. Brewery tap for Breconshire Brewery idyllically located by the River Usk. LD3 9AL

Brecon

Robin Smithett

SARAH SIDDONS - High Street. Tel: 01874 610666. Atmospheric town centre pub offering weekday lunches. Named after the Victorian actress who was born here. LD3 7AP

Shopping

Most of the major stores you'd expect to find in a town of this size, many of them in the new Bethel Square shopping precinct by the main car park. Plenty of outdoor activity shops -a good place to buy that new pair of walking boots you've been promising yourself. The indoor market dates from 1840 and markets are held on Tuesdays and Fridays with the addition of lively farmer's markets on the second Saturday of each month. MORRISONS, CO-OP and ALDI supermarkets. Three good outlets for secondhand books: ANDREW MORTON'S on Lion Street, BOOKS, MAPS & PRINTS on The Struet and BRECON ANTIQUES on High Street.

Things to Do

TOURIST INFORMATION CENTRE - Cattle Market Car Park. Tel: 01874 622485. LD3 9DA
THEATR BRYCHEINIOG - Canal Wharf. Tel: 01874 611622. LD3 7EW
BRECKNOCK MUSEUM - Captain's Walk. Tel: 01874 624121. Open daily. Admission charge. Local history, natural history, plus varied exhibitions. LD3 7DS
BRECON CATHEDRAL - Tel: 01874 625222. Former Benedictine priory refurbished by George Gilbert Scott in 1872. Tithe barn heritage centre and restaurant. LD3 9DP
SOUTH WALES BORDERERS AND MONMOUTHSHIRE REGIMENTAL MUSEUM - The Barracks. Tel: 01874 613310. Open daily Apr-Sept, weekdays Oct-Mar. Admission charge. The history of two famous regiments over 300 years. LD3 7PY
DRAGONFLY CRUISES - Canal Wharf. Tel: 07831 685222. Public boat trips from Brecon out to Brynich Lock and back. LD3 7EW
BIKE HIRE - Bi-Ped Cycles, Free Street. Tel: 01874 622296. www.bipedcycles.co.uk LD3 9AF
BRECONSHIRE BREWERY - Ffrwdgrech Industrial Estate. Tel: 01874 623731. Shop and tours of this micro-brewery located about a mile to the west of the town centre. LD3 8LA

Connections

BUSES - alas no 'deep panting' Pannier tanks make their wheezy way up from Newport on the incomparable Brecon & Merthyr line via Torpantau and Pontsticill Junction, nor is there a rail link, as once with Hereford via Hay-on-Wye. In their place buses link Brecon with Crickhowell, Abergavenny and intermediate villages. Also to Hay-on-Wye, Hereford and Merthyr. Tel: 0871 200 2233.
TAXIS - Brecon Taxis Tel: 01874 623444. AA Cabs. Tel: 01874 622288.

Hire Bases

ANDERSEN BOATS - Middlewich, Trent & Mersey Canal, Map 29. Tel: 01606 833668. *www.andersenboats.com* CW10 9BQ

ANGLO WELSH - Bunbury, Shropshire Union Canal, Map 13. Trevor, Llangollen Canal, Map 26. Tel: 0117 304 1122. *www.anglowelsh.co.uk* CW6 9QB

BEACON PARK BOATS - Llanfoist, Monmouthshire & Brecon Canal, Map 42. Tel: 01873 858277. *www.beaconparkboats.com* NP7 9NG

BETTISFIELD BOATS - Bettisfield, Llangollen Canal, Map 22. Tel: 01948 710398. *www.bettisfieldboats.com* SY13 2LJ

BLACK PRINCE NARROWBOATS - Chirk, Llangollen Canal, Map 25. Tel: 01527 575115. *www.black-prince.com* LL14 5AD

CAMBRIAN CRUISERS - Pencelli, Monmouthshire & Brecon Canal, Map 46. Tel: 01874 665315. *www.cambriancruisers.co.uk* LD3 7LJ

CASTLE NARROWBOATS - Gilwern, Monmouthshire & Brecon Canal, Map 43. Tel: 01873 830001. *www.castlenarrowboats.co.uk* NP7 0EP

CHESHIRE CAT NARROWBOAT HOLIDAYS - Overwater Marina, Shropshire Union Canal, Map 9. Tel: 07867 790195. *www.cheshirecatnarrowboats.co.uk* CW5 8AY

COUNTRY CRAFT - Llangynidr, Monmouthshire & Brecon Canal, Map 45. Tel: 01874 730850. *www.country-craft.co.uk* NP8 1ND

COUNTRYWIDE CRUISERS - Brewood, Shropshire Union Canal, Map 2. Tel: 01902 850166. *www.countrywide-cruisers.com* ST19 9BG

Boating Directory

CREST NARROWBOATS - Chirk, Llangollen Canal, Map 25. Tel: 01691 774558. *www.crestnarrowboats.co.uk* LL14 5AD

EMPRESS HOLIDAYS - Nantwich, Shropshire Union Canal, Map 11. Tel: 01270 624075. *www.empressholidays.com* CW5 8LA

CHAS HARDERN - Beeston, Shropshire Union Canal, Map13. Tel: 01829 732595. *www.chashardern.co.uk* CW6 9NH

MAESTERMYN HIRE CRUISERS - Whittington, Llangollen Canal, Map 24. Tel: 01691 662424. *www.maestermyn.co.uk* SY11 4NU

MIDDLEWICH NARROWBOATS - Middlewich, Trent & Mersey Canal, Map 29. Tel: 01606 832460. *www.middlewichboats.co.uk* CW10 9BD

MID WALES NARROWBOATS - Whittington, Llangollen Canal, Map 24. Tel: 01691 650243. *www.maestermyn.co.uk* SY11 4NU

NAPTON NARROWBOATS - Autherley Junction, Shropshire Union Canal, Map 1. Tel: 01902 789942. *www.watertravel.co.uk* WV9 5HW

NORBURY WHARF - Norbury Junction, Shropshire Union Canal, Map 5.Tel: 01785 284292. *www.norburywharfltd.co.uk* ST20 0PN

RED LINE BOATS - Goytre Wharf, Monmouthshire & Brecon Canal, Map 41. Tel: 01873 880516. *www.redlineboats.co.uk* NP7 9EW

ROAD HOUSE HIRE - Gilwern, Monmouthshire & Brecon Canal, Map 43. Tel: 01873 830240. *www.narrowboats-wales.co.uk* NP7 0AS

UK BOAT HIRE - Anderton, Trent & Mersey Canal, Map 31. Tel: 0845 126 4098. *www.ukboathire.com* CW9 6AJ

UK BOAT HIRE - Goytre Wharf, Monmouthshire & Brecon Canal, Map 41. Tel: 0845 126 4098. *www.ukboathire.com* NP7 9EW

UK BOAT HIRE - Wrenbury, Llangollen Canal, Map 19. Tel: 0845 126 4098 or 01270 780544 *www.ukboathire.com* CW5 8HG

VIKING AFLOAT - Whitchurch, Llangollen Canal, Map 20. Tel: 0845 126 4098 or 01948 662012 *www.viking-afloat.com* SY13 3AA

WELSH LADY - Whittington, Llangollen Canal, Map 24. Tel: 01691 662424. *www.maestermyn.co.uk* SY11 4NU

Horse Drawn Cruises

BYWATER HOLIDAYS - Tel: 07971 303416 *www.bywaterholidays.co.uk* Skippered horse-drawn boating holidays on the Montgomery Canal: daytime aboard; nights in small hotel/guest house accommodation.

Day Boat Hire*

BEACON PARK DAY BOATS - Brecon, Monmouthshire & Brecon Canal, Map 47. Tel: 0800 612 2890.

LLANGOLLEN WHARF - Llangollen, Llangollen Canal, Map 27. Tel: 01978 860702.

MIDWAY BOATS - Barbridge, Shropshire Union Canal, Map 12. Tel: 01270 528482.

NANTWICH CANAL CENTRE - Nantwich, Shropshire Union Canal, Map 11. Tel: 01270 625122.

* A number of the hire bases listed opposite also offer day hire.

Boatyards

ANDERTON MARINA (ABC) - Anderton, Trent & Mersey Canal, Map 31. Tel: 01606 79642. CW9 6AJ

AQUEDUCT MARINA - Church Minshull, Middlewich Branch, Map 28. Tel: 01928 701098. CW5 6DX

BARBRIDGE MARINA/MIDWAY BOATS - Barbridge, Shropshire Union Canal, Map 12. Tel: 01270 528482. CW5 6BE

BETTON MILL WHARF - Market Drayton, Shropshire Union Canal, Map 8. Tel: 01691 656269. TF9 1HH

BLACKWATER MEADOW MARINA (ABC) - Ellesmere, Llangollen Canal, Map 23. Tel: 01691 624391. SY12 9DD

BOAT BUILDING SERVICES - Stoak, Shropshire Union Canal, Map 17. Tel: 0151 357 1949. CH65 4AJ

CHIRK MARINE - Chirk, Llangollen Canal, Map 25. Tel: 01691 774558. LL14 5AD

HERON'S REST MARINA - Llangattock, Monmouthshire & Brecon Canal, Map 44. Tel: 0845 230 2814. NP8 1HS

HOLIDAYS AFLOAT - Market Drayton, Shropshire Union Canal, Map 8. Tel: 01630 652937. TF9 1HW

KINGS LOCK - Middlewich, Trent & Mersey Canal, Map 29. Tel: 01606 833633. CW10 0JJ

Top of Hurleston Locks

Karen Tanguy

MAESBURY MARINE SERVICES - Maesbury, Montgomery Canal, Map 33. Tel: 01691 679963. SY10 8BB

NANTWICH CANAL CENTRE - Nantwich, Shropshire Union Canal, Map 11. Tel: 01270 625122. CW5 8LB

ORCHARD MARINA - Northwich, Trent & Mersey Canal, Map 30. Tel: 01606 42082. CW9 7RG

ORWELLS BOATYARD - Market Drayton, Shropshire Union Canal, Map 8. Tel: 01630 652472. TF9 4BH

OVERWATER MARINA - Audlem, Shropshire Union, Map 9. Tel: 01270 812748. CW5 8AY

SWANLEY BRIDGE MARINA - Swanley, Llangollen Canal, Map 18. Tel: 01270 524571. CW5 8NR

TALBOT WHARF - Market Drayton, Shropshire Union Canal, Map 8. Tel: 01630 652641. TF9 1HW

TATTENHALL MARINA - Tattenhall, Shropshire Union Canal, Map 14. Tel: 01889 883713. CH3 9BD

VENETIAN MARINE - Cholmondeston, Shropshire Union Canal Middlewich Branch, Map 12. Tel: 01270 528251. CW5 6DD

WHIXALL MARINE - Whixall, Llangollen Canal, Map 22. Tel: 01948 880420. SY13 2QP

WINCHAM WHARF - Lostock Gralam, Trent & Mersey Canal, Map 31. Tel: 01606 44672. CW9 7NT

How To Use The Maps

There are forty-seven numbered maps whose layout is shown by the Route Planner inside the front cover. Maps 1 to 17 cover the 'main line' of the Shropshire Union Canal between Autherley Junction (Wolverhampton) and Ellesmere Port; Maps18 to 27 cover the Llangollen Canal from Hurleston Junction (Nantwich) to Horseshoe Falls (Llangollen); Maps 28 to 31 cover the Middlewich Branch of the Shropshire Union together with the Trent & Mersey Canal between Middlewich and Anderton (Northwich); Maps 32 to 39 cover the Montgomery Canal from Frankton to Newtown (users should note that this canal is only partially navigable at present); Maps 40 to 47 cover the Monmouthshire & Brecon Canal from Pontnewydd (Cwmbran) to Brecon. The maps are easily read in either direction. The simplest way of progressing from map to map is to proceed to the next map numbered from the edge of the map you are on. Figures quoted at the top of each map refer to distance per map, locks per map and average cruising time. An alternative indication of timings from centre to centre can be found on the Route Planner. Obviously, cruising times vary with the nature of your boat and the number of crew at your disposal, so quoted times should be taken only as an estimate. Neither do times quoted take into account any delays which might occur at lock flights in high season.

Using The Text

Each map is accompanied by a route commentary. Regular readers will already be familiar with our somewhat irreverent approach. But we 'tell it as we find it', in the belief that the users of this guide will find this attitude more

Information

valuable than a strict adherence to the tourist publicity line: twenty-eight years of research and feedback and nearly half a million sales suggest that you broadly agree!

Towpath Walking

The simplest way to go canal exploring is on foot. It costs largely nothing and you are free to concentrate on the passing scene; something that boaters are not always at liberty to do. As usual the maps show the quality of the towpath, and whilst it does vary from area to area, none of it should prove problematical for anyone inured to the vicissitudes of country walking. We advocate the use of public transport to facilitate 'one-way' itineraries but stress the advisability of checking up to date details on the telephone numbers quoted. Incidentally, we recommend employing public transport for the outward leg before returning on foot, that way you won't need to worry unduly about hurrying back to catch your bus or train.

Towpath Cycling

Cycling canal towpaths is an increasingly popular activity, but one which British Waterways - the body responsible for the upkeep of the bulk of Britain's navigable inland waterways - is only slowly coming to terms with. At present it is necessary for cyclists wishing to use towpaths to

acquire a free of charge permit from a British Waterways office - see opposite.

Boating

Boating on inland waterways is an established, though relatively small, facet of the UK holiday industry. There are over 30,000 privately owned boats registered on the canals, but in addition to these, numerous firms offer boats for hire. These range from small operators with half a dozen boats to sizeable fleets run by companies with several bases.

Most hire craft have all the creature comforts you are likely to expect. In the excitement of planning a boating holiday you may give scant thought to the contents of your hire boat, but at the end of a hard day's boating such matters take on more significance, and a well equipped, comfortable boat, large enough to accommodate your crew with something to spare, can make the difference between a good holiday and an indifferent one.

Traditionally, hire boats are booked out by the week or fortnight, though many firms now offer more flexible short breaks or extended weeks. All reputable hire firms give newcomers tuition in boat handling and lock working, and first-timers soon find themselves adapting to the pace of things.

Navigational Advice

LOCKS are part of the charm of canal cruising, but they are potentially dangerous environments for children, pets and careless adults. Use of them should be methodical and unhurried, whilst special care should be exercised in rain, frost and snow when slippery hazards abound. We lack space for detailed instructions on lock operation: trusting that if you own a boat you will, by definition, already be experienced in canal cruising; whilst first-time hire boaters should be given tuition in the operation of locks before they set out.

The majority of locks included in this guide are of the narrow variety. However, on the Shropshire Union Canal north of Nantwich they are widebeam and capable of accommodating two narrowboats side by side. There are 'staircase' locks at Bunbury, Grindley Brook and Frankton where adjacent chambers share common gates. When working uphill the upper chamber must be full so that the water in it can be released to fill the lower chamber. Going downhill, the lower chamber must be empty to enable the water from the upper chamber to flow into it.

LIFT BRIDGES are a feature of the Llangollen, Montgomery and Monmouthshire & Brecon canals. Great care should be taken to ensure that the bridge platform remains firmly upright as your boat passes through. Lift bridges at Wrenbury (Llangollen Canal) and Talybont (Mon & Brec) are electrically operated using a British Waterways sanitary key.

MOORING on the canals featured in this guide is per usual practice - ie on the towpath side, away from sharp bends, bridge-holes and narrows. An 'open' bollard symbol represents visitor mooring sites; either as designated specifically by British Waterways, the Shropshire Union Canal Society or, in some cases, as suggested by our personal experience.

PRIVATE NAVIGATIONS which connect with British Waterways canals covered in this guide are the Manchester Ship Canal at Ellesmere Port (Map 17) and the River Dee at Chester (Map 16). Hire boaters will not be permitted to enter either of these waterways; private pleasure craft may use the MSC only if they comply with a number of strict conditions, such as Third Party insurance and a Certificate of Seaworthiness. Full details from the Harbour Master, Manchester Ship Canal, Queen Elizabeth II Dock, Eastham, Wirral CH62 0BB. Tel: 0151 327 1461.

The Dee below Chester is a tidal, fast flowing river not recommended for use by canal craft. The Upper Dee, however, flows charmingly through the Cheshire countryside and may be reached (by prior arrangement with BW - Tel: 01606 723800) via the Dee Branch. To boat the Dee one must also contact Chester City Council, The Forum, Chester CH1 2HS. Tel: 01244 324324.

CLOSURES (or 'stoppages' in canal parlance) traditionally occur on the inland waterways between November and April, during which time most of the heavy maintenance work is undertaken. Occasionally, however, an emergency stoppage, or perhaps water restriction, may be imposed at short notice, closing part of the route you intend to use. Up-to-date details are usually available from hire bases and British Waterways provide a recorded message on 01923 201401.

Useful Contacts

BRITISH WATERWAYS - Wales & Border Counties, Navigation Road, Northwich, Cheshire CW8 1BH. Tel: 01606 723800.
Monmouthshire & Brecon Canal - Canal Office, The Wharf, Govilon, Abergavenny NP7 9NY. Tel: 01873 830328.
www.waterscape.com
British Waterways operate a central emergency telephone service. Tel: 0800 479 9947.

Societies

The Inland Waterways Association was founded in 1946 to campaign for retention of the canal system. Many routes have now been open to pleasure boaters may not have been so but for this organisation. Membership details may be obtained from: Inland Waterways Association, Island House, Moor Road, Chesham, Bucks HP5 1WA Tel: 01494 783453 www.waterways.org.uk

Acknowledgements

Many thanks to Brian Collings for the 'Great Western' inspired cover; to Toby and Ruth Bryant of Troll Publishing; to Karen Tanguy for research, pre-production and photography; to Robin Smithett for additional photography; and to all at Hawksworths of Uttoxeter who organised the preparation and printing of this edition. Mapping reproduced by permission of Ordnance Survey on behalf of Her Majesty's Stationery Office, Crown Copyright 100033032. Every effort has been made to make this guide as up to date and accurate as possible, but Troll Publishing cannot be held responsible for errors and omissions and their consequences.

Nine Good Reasons for Exploring the Canals with Pearsons

8th edition - ISBN 978 0 9 5491168 3

9th edition - ISBN 978 0 9559041 1 0

8th edition - ISBN 978-0-9559041-2-7

8th edition - ISBN 978 0 9 5491169 0

6th edition - ISBN 0 9549116 5 2

7th edition - ISBN 978 0 9 549 1166 9

7th edition - ISBN 978 0 955904 1 0 3

3rd edition - ISBN 0 9545383 4 X

2nd edition - ISBN 978 0 9 5491167 6

Pearson's Canal Companions are published by Troll Publishing. They are widely available from hire bases, boatyards, canal shops, good bookshops, via the internet and the Inland Waterways Association. For further details contact Troll on 01788 546692 or canalcompanions@trollpublishing.co.uk